D1510784

STEPHEN POLLAN'S
FOOLPROOF GUIDE
TO BUYING A HOME

STEPHEN M. POLLAN
& MARK LEVINE

ILLUSTRATIONS BY BETSY BAYTOS

A FIRESIDE BOOK
PUBLISHED BY SIMON & SCHUSTER

FIRESIDE
Rockefeller Center
1230 Avenue of the Americas
New York, NY 10020

Designed by Irving Perkins Associates

Manufactured in the United States of America

1   3   5   7   9   10   8   6   4   2

Library of Congress Cataloging-in-Publication Data

Pollan, Stephen M.
Stephen Pollan's foolproof guide to buying a home / Stephen M.
Pollan & Mark Levine: illustrations by Betsy Baytos.
p.   cm.
"A fireside book."
1. House buying—United States.   I. Levine, Mark, date.
II. Title.
HD255.P65   1997
643'. 12–dc21   96-40870
CIP

ISBN 0–684–80228–7

CONTENTS

INTRODUCTION

Over the past four decades I've played a part in the purchase of literally hundreds of homes. While in most cases I've served as the attorney for either the buyer or the seller, in six of those instances my wife and I were the buyers, and in at least another half-dozen instances my children and parents were the buyers. Having gone through the process so often, as both a professional and as a private citizen, I've learned there's more to the home-buying process than just the financial, legal, and procedural. At least as important, if not most important of all, is the emotional element.

I have seen otherwise intelligent and successful individuals paralyzed when it comes to buying a home, because the dominant emotions present in the process are fear and self-doubt. That's a shame.

The purchase of a home should be an exciting and exhilarating process. Sure, it's a lot of work and the sums of money involved are awesome. But buying a home is one of the few times we can enhance the financial and spiritual aspects of our lives, as well as the lives of our loved ones. The purchase of a first home starts you on the road to financial security and growth. The purchase of a home, regardless of your age, can lift your spirits to heights never reached before. It can nurture, shelter, and give focus to your life. It can even accelerate the binding of relationships.

But too many people let fear get in the way. Everyone is afraid of overcommitting financially, afraid of putting down semipermanent roots, afraid of making a mistake, afraid of being afraid. And I do mean everyone. I've represented Middle Eastern royalty, professional athletes, Hollywood film stars, influential politicians, Australian adventurers, and hotshot Wall Street bankers, and every last one of them demonstrated the identical fears and doubts that strike the widow buying a retirement home with some of her limited assets or the young couple tightening their belts to buy their first home.

What's just as extraordinary is that these fears are easily overcome. In fact, that's a large part of what I do with my clients—remove their fear. All it takes is knowledge and confidence.

People come into my office, scared and ill at ease, and by the end of the home-buying process they're transformed into self-assured individuals. (An added blessing is that the knowledge they acquire along the way helps them the rest of their lives.) I simply tell them what to expect, how to overcome obstacles, and what they need to know. Then, I boost their confidence by being there, either in person or over the telephone, whenever they need me.

Obviously, I can't offer that kind of personalized attention to every reader. But in this book I've come as close as possible by breaking the home-buying process down into an easily understood series of steps. These steps are accompanied by hundreds of tips and warnings. These are just the sort of suggestions I'd be offering if you were my client, my son, or my mother. I think this approach brings total clarity to the home-buying process; and I know it works.

I've used just this approach to buy two suburban single-family homes, an urban cooperative apartment, two summer homes, and a weekend home in the country for my wife and me. I've used this approach to help all four of my children and their spouses buy homes. I've used this approach to help my parents buy a retirement home. And I have used this approach to help literally hundreds of clients from every background and economic level.

My advice works for those buying for the first time, stepping up to a larger home, purchasing a weekend or vacation home, or acquiring a retirement home. It works for co-ops, condos, single-family homes, or multifamily dwellings. When appropriate, I've offered specific tips for all those variations.

That doesn't mean this book replaces competent professional advice. I can offer you the information and confidence you need, but only a caring adviser with first-hand knowledge of your particular needs, wants, and circumstances can formulate the kind of customized transaction that you'll learn about in these pages.

My goal is to replace your fears and doubts with knowledge and confidence. And the first step in the transformation is to turn the page.

——Stephen M. Pollan

How to Use This Book

This book is designed to be used, not just read. The project of buying a home has been broken down into a series of eight stages. Each of these stages has then been broken down into an easy to follow series of steps. Tips and warnings about each step are also provided. Before acting on any individual step, read through the book once, including all the tips and warnings. Then, go back to the beginning and proceed through the process, using the book as a guide. When you complete a step, check the box labeled "Done," and move on to the next step. Avoid the temptation to jump ahead or to do things out of order. The stages and steps have been designed to build on one another and have been written based on my more than thirty years of experience going through this exact process.

—*Stephen M. Pollan*

ESTABLISHING YOUR GOALS AND DETERMINING YOUR AFFORDABILITY

One of the biggest mistakes home buyers make is to go out into the market without a clear-cut understanding of their needs and wants or their financial resources. That's why the first step in the home-buying process is one of self-analysis.

1 **Assess your feelings about your current dwelling.** Make a list of all the things you love—and hate—about your current home. Include everything you can think of, from its proximity to the best Thai restaurant in town—which you love—to the neighbors you see over the back fence every day—whom you hate. When you're done, rewrite the list, putting the most important items at the top and the less important items on the bottom.

☐ **Done**

Tip 1.1: Be ruthless in your assessments. After all, this list will help you determine your priorities— priorities that paint a picture not only of your dream house, but where that house should be located for optimum happiness.

2 **Decide how much time you're willing to spend commuting.** In general, the farther you live from your workplace, the more house you can get for your money. Some people are willing to take on a long commute if it means returning each day to a house they love. Others are willing to forgo their dream house in favor of the convenience of a short trip. Only you can decide which pattern works best for you.

☐ **Done**

3 Examine your feelings about privacy.

Some folks love yakking it up with the neighbors and feeling part of a community; others prefer to keep to themselves and are horrified by the notion of having to see, talk, or spend time with anyone around and about the neighborhood. Assessing your desire for privacy will help you determine where you'll wind up living and the kind of house you're likely to buy.

☐ **Done**

Tip 3.1: Decide how many windows you want. Light, fresh air, and/or a stunning view can make or break a home. However, remember to factor in your requirements for privacy.

Tip 3.2: North, south, east, west—don't forget that exposure is a significant factor. While light and weather vary throughout the year, the ideal exposure is generally south.

4 **Determine the size house you'll need.** Study your family and its living habits. Are you planning to have another child? Do the kids and adults have separate bathrooms? Does everyone eat dinner together in the kitchen? Is this house for the future? Are you trying to reach beyond your grasp in anticipation of the future?

☐ **Done**

Tip 4.1: A home should have as many rooms as you need—plus one. This will save you the expense of converting a basement or garage, and will virtually ensure you won't in any way destroy the design, integrity, or character of your home.

Tip 4.2: It's better to buy a home with lots of small rooms than one with a few large rooms. More rooms means more privacy.

5 **Consider the importance of shopping in your life.** It goes without saying that you'll want to be close to a supermarket and a drugstore, but there are other criteria you need to take into consideration. Do you view shopping as a chore or as a hobby? Are you a walker or would you die without your car? And what specialty stores and/or restaurants do you require to be nearby to feel life is truly worth living? How important is proximity to public transportation, museums, the library, and the post office?

☐ **Done**

6 Factor in schools only if they're necessary now.

A good school district can add to the value of a home. But there's no point paying a mint to live in a superior school district if your kids aren't of school age yet. Just because a school district has a great rep now doesn't mean the quality of education will remain high in the future when it's your kids' turn to walk the hallowed halls of K–12 academia.

☐ **Done**

7 **Banish the phrase "energy efficiency" from your vocabulary.** It might sound like a good impetus for buying, but the truth is no one knows what the energy situation will be in fifteen, ten, or even five years. If you're truly concerned about saving energy, invest in a thick wool sweater and turn the thermostat down.

☐ **Done**

Tip 7.1: There's one caveat: assess your heating and cooling needs carefully if you're planning to move to an area that requires extraordinary air conditioning or heating to be comfortable.

8 Remember exterior appearance does matter.

Any house you look at should be in keeping with the character of the neighborhood if you want it at least to maintain its value.

☐ **Done**

9 **Determine the importance of the outdoor area surrounding your home.** Some folks love being outside and thrive on planting, landscaping, and the like. Others consider time spent in the yard a form of torture. Make sure you're in touch with your own likes and dislikes.

☐ **Done**

10 Consider your needs for storage space.

A home is more than just living space—it's also the place where you stash all your family's "stuff."

☐ **Done**

Tip 10.1: Calculate the number of closets you'll need, assuming you'll require one for each member of the family—plus two more for linens and coats. You might need more if you or anyone else in your clan is a chronic pack rat.

Tip 10.2: Decide whether you really need a basement. Sure, it can be convenient for storage, but a crawl space works just as well. Don't be suckered into paying more for a finished basement, since it will not add to the resale value of a home—rooms created below ground never do. However, if you need a place for young children, the basement as an auxiliary room may be a priority.

11

Decide whether you want an old or a new home. Brand-new split-levels and 100-year-old Victorians have their own pros and cons. Which you aim for depends on your specific needs and wants.

☐ **Done**

Tip 11.1: If it's important to you to live in a space unsullied by previous residents, look at new homes. In general, they're easier to buy, if only because more can be seen by the naked eye. In addition, you'll be protected by the latest regulations of the local building department and your state's construction code and will be able to take advantage of the latest in insulation and climate-control technology. Newer homes also tend to be cheaper to furnish, since many come with wall-to-wall carpeting and window treatments, as well as more appliances and fix-

tures. It is also enticing that you're likely to be surrounded by other new-home owners, which could foster a sense of neighborliness and provide the foundation for a true community.

Warning 11.2: There are some cons when it comes to buying "new," primarily the risk that comes with buying in an area where a neighborhood has not yet been established. Another drawback is that homes in a development may lack individuality. You'll also only be able to guess at what your heating and electrical costs will be (not to mention your real estate taxes), and if you're buying from a model or a blueprint, you'll be completely in the dark as to what role location, weather, and other external factors will play. When you see the plans on paper, your unit may be overlooking a lake. When it's built you may find yourself with a gorgeous view of the interstate.

Warning 11.3: But old homes have drawbacks, too. Maintaining "character" requires time and money, as does the

cost of upkeep to older structural and building systems. It's also not uncommon for neighbors in older, established neighborhoods to ignore the new kids on the block. In addition, sellers of old homes are usually quite adept at covering the house's flaws, of which there are sure to be a few.

12 **Decide what type of structure you want to live in.** There are four primary types: detached single-family houses, attached houses, multifamily houses, and apartments.

☐ **Done**

Tip 12. 1: The most popular type of structure to own in America is the detached single-family house, situated on its own piece of property. It offers the greatest amount of space and privacy. That's why it's so coveted: it's one of the quintessential aspects of "the American Dream."

Warning 12.2: However, detached single-family homes are also the most expensive type of structure. That's understandable: you are not only paying for the aforementioned space and privacy, but also the entire heating and cooling costs. In addition, you are solely responsible for the cost of maintaining the structure and property, which can be expensive as well as time-consuming. And there's no tenant to defray costs. Yet for most Americans, the privacy and space are worth it.

Tip 12.3: If privacy isn't *numero uno* on your list of priorities, you might be quite happy in an attached home. These include single-family dwellings (townhouses, brownstones, and row houses), as well as two-family houses and "quadruplexes." Attached homes share a common wall——or two——with neighbors. They're cheaper to purchase as well as to maintain and feature the added incentive of lower utility costs.

Warning 12.4: However, attached houses tend to have smaller outdoor areas. If you're a fanatical gardener, or like animals, think twice before buying one.

Tip 12.5: Multifamily homes (two- or three-family houses) may not be the most attractive to look at, but they do offer a financial opportunity to the owners, who can rent out units to help cover the cost of the mortgage and maintenance. Rental properties also guarantee various tax breaks which can be immensely helpful. Also important, multifamily homes offer independence to the owner in a way apartments do not: you're free to choose your neighbors and make any and all alterations you want.

Warning 12.6: Multi-family homes are more expensive to buy than attached homes. They can also lack privacy, and there is additional legal exposure that comes with the turf, not to mention the hassles associated with becoming a landlord.

Tip 12.7: Looking to save bucks? Consider buying an apartment. It is the least expensive dwelling to purchase and maintain, and is usually conveniently located near shopping and culture as well.

Warning 12.8: Pack rats and apartments do not mix. While there are great advantages to apartment dwelling, one common disadvantage is lack of storage space. Apartments may also lack privacy, depending on the floor plan and acoustics of the building. Another caveat is a view of the courtyard: it can be like living next door to a garbage dump.

Tip 12.9: A relatively new type of dwelling space is the PUD, or Planned Unit Development, in which developers purchase a huge tract of land and create an entire community from the ground up, with all types of residences, stores, and even schools. PUD home prices tend to be lower than those for similar homes in conventional areas, and they do offer convenience.

Warning 12.10: However, the future of PUDs is iffy. Many are not doing well, and one major drawback to them is that if you choose to do anything outside the community, their major advantage—proximity to services—flies out the window. PUDs take years to develop, and the developers need to be sophisticated and well heeled. Just because a company is successful at manufacturing a certain product doesn't mean it will be successful at building a community.

13

Choose the form of home owner-ship that best suits your needs. There are five primary types: fee simple, condominium, cooperative, association, and partnership, each with its own pros and cons.

☐ **Done**

Tip 13.1: Fee simple is the most common form of home ownership in America. It's not hard to under-stand why. It means you own the building and the property it stands on, from one property line to another. It's the most private and secure form of home ownership. It also presents the fewest com-plications when dealing with the professionals involved in home purchase—namely, attorneys, inspectors, builders, and brokers.

Warning 13.2: However, if money is a concern, fee simple might not be the way to go—it's the most expensive form of home ownership.

Tip 13.3: If your wish is to fully own your home but jointly own common facilities—such as lawns, gardens, walkways, stairs, elevators, etc.—consider buying a condominium, or "condo." These are usually multi-family attached dwellings. Condos tend to be cheaper than fee-simple homes—since the costs of some areas are shared—yet offer all their tax advantages. In addition, condo owners often have more amenities and facilities—swimming pools, workout rooms, hiking paths, tennis courts—at their disposal than the owners of single standing homes.

Warning 13.4: However, condos don't maintain their value as well as fee-simple homes. Also, you'll be required to pay a common area charge to maintain the upkeep of the communal property, as well as applicable taxes. Decision making is communal as well. Owners decide together when to raise or lower maintenance fees, for instance. In addition, the purchase of a condo is more complicated than the purchase of a fee-simple home, requiring you and your attorney to examine the bylaws and the declaration of development to find out about your

rights to do construction if you so desire. Most condo bylaws feature a right of first refusal, which means the home must first be offered to the board of managers. Condo boards also require you give them power of attorney to represent you in areas of common interest.

Tip 13.5: Cheaper than condominiums, cooperatives are an option worth considering. In a co-op, you own shares in a corporation, which in turn owns the building you live in. Most co-ops are apartment houses and complexes. For that reason, it's important that prospective co-op buyers hire an accountant to examine the building's financial status. Many co-ops have balloon mortgages potentially requiring you to fork over a very large final payment when the note comes due; however, what usually happens is that another mortgage is obtained instead. This underlying mortgage could cause owners' costs to skyrocket, but it also ensures you get more square footage for your dollar when buying a co-op than when buying a condo.

Warning 13.6: Co-ops often have higher maintenance costs than condos, since the monthly fee usually includes upkeep of the building as well as the mortgage payment. Co-op payments also have a tendency to increase faster than those for condos, since many of the charges— such as heating, labor, insurance—are subject to inflation and cost-of-living increases.

Warning 13.7: The greatest disadvantage to co-ops is that they're managed by a board of residents. Buyers must be approved by the board, which is trying to ferret out any potential nonpaying stockholder while simultaneously attempting to maintain a real or imagined culture within the building. This preservation of "ambience" can lead to rampant snobbism.

Tip 13.8: Another form of home ownership, albeit rare, is membership in an association. You own your home and the land it stands on, but share ownership of a communal recreation area, like a beach or park. Most associations involve single-family homes located in vacation or resort areas. They are designed to ensure the members have privacy from vacationers and day-trippers. While membership fees are charged, they tend to be lower than those you'd pay to belong to a private club.

Warning 13.9: However, associations do require you to surrender some privacy, and you'll be paying fees for a communal area whether you use that area or not. In addition, some associations have strict architectural rules that could interfere with plans for renovation and new construction.

Tip 13.10: If you're single, you may want to investigate another form of ownership known as partnership, in which two or more individuals share down payment, mortgage, and maintenance costs. This can be the perfect arrangement if you've got your eye on an older, larger home that easily lends itself to being split up into two distinct residences. Since real estate partnerships can be complicated arrangements, make sure you know everything about your potential partner beforehand, including his or her full financial history, and make sure that an experienced attorney draws up the agreement, so it covers such areas as rights, responsibilities, and division of amenities.

Retirement Home Buyer's Tip 13.11: If you're retiring, think about moving from a single-family detached home to attached housing—either a co-op, condo, or an association. Retirement-specific developments are also worth considering, since their recreational and educational activities cater to older Americans. They also frequently restrict the access of children and pets, creating a quieter environment.

Retirement Home Buyer's Tip 13.12: Retirement developments are often wonderful . . . for a time. When everyone is an active senior, playing golf or tennis or swimming in the pool, they can be fabulous. But they tend to age as a unit. As the community gets older, wheelchairs can replace golf carts and ambulettes can replace sports cars. That can be comforting, but it also can be petrifying. A mixed community may be noisier, but it will never grow sterile.

14

Carefully classify your goals. Label your goals as either essential, desirable, or a dream. Essentials go at the top of the list; dreams go at the bottom. This ranking of goals will help you to remain objective while house hunting, and will serve as a reminder of what is truly important to you. You'll need it if you're to survive the shark-infested waters of the real estate market.

☐ **Done**

Vacation Home Buyer's Tip 14.1: If you're looking to buy a vacation property, there are other considerations you need to examine. Are you planning to have this house become your primary residence one day? How far are you willing to travel to get to this house: a six-hour drive; a two-hour plane ride? Is the house just for you, or do you plan to rent it out for part of the year?

15

Figure out your own home affordability. With your goals prioritized, it's time to figure out how much you can afford to pay to achieve them.

☐ **Done**

Warning 15.1: Others—namely lenders, brokers, family, and friends—will suggest you figure out your affordability based on a "traditional" formula, such as taking your gross yearly income and multiplying it by two and a half. Don't listen to them. There's only one person qualified to assess what you can and can't afford, and that's you.

16

Look at your affordability as a monthly expense. Rather than focusing on the total you'll be paying for a home, look at your affordability as a monthly expense. Rather than saying, "I can afford to pay $150,000 for a house," consider what you can—and are willing—to spend monthly on living expenses. That's what it will end up being anyway if you're going to be obtaining a mortgage, as most buyers do, since the bank will judge your ability to carry a mortgage by comparing the monthly payment against your monthly income.

☐ **Done**

17

Determine how much you're spending now. To see how much you'll be able to spend on a home in the future, look first at how much you're spending on shelter and other expenses now.

☐ **Done**

Tip 17.1: Most people can only account for 75 percent of where their money goes. To track down the missing 25 percent, look at your monthly credit-card bills, the checks you've written to cash, and your ATM receipts.

18 Decide what you're willing to give up to own a home.

If you're spending $1,000 a month now for rent, you can spend at least that much on a mortgage payment. You can stretch your affordability by giving up other expenses or trimming them, then shifting the money saved to your mortgage payment. Be somewhat liberal in determining what you can afford, as your ability to spend will increase as you pay down your debt and your salary increases.

☐ **Done**

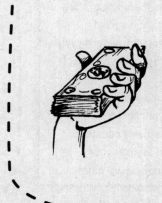

Vacation Home Buyer's Tip 18.1: When calculating vacation-home affordability, be aware that cutting back in areas such as weekend dining and entertainment won't be sufficient to help you raise the money for a monthly payment. That means you may need to turn to your investments or retirement savings. I think this is usually okay as long as the mortgage payment is a fixed amount, allowing you to take advantage of inflation (as prices rise over the years, your payment remains constant). Hopefully, your income will outpace your expenses and you'll be able to start saving again. A well-located second home can be a marvelous investment.

Retirement Home Buyer's Tip 18.2: Older Americans shouldn't factor in too many expense cuts when it comes to figuring out their monthly affordability. Chances are slim your income is going to grow, while odds are your other expenses—particularly health care costs—may rise.

19

Factor taxes into your monthly affordability. Make sure to include the tax break afforded by mortgage payments. Under current tax law, the interest portion of your payment is deductible. That means if you determine you can afford $1,000 in rent, and you're in the 28 percent tax bracket, you can actually afford to pay $1,280 for a mortgage payment. Why? Because in the early years of a mortgage, what you're primarily paying off is interest, thus your payments are almost totally tax deductible.

☐ **Done**

Tip 19.1: If you're buying your first home, consider increasing the number of deductions on your W-4 tax withholding form. That way, you'll have more money in your paycheck to pay your monthly mortgage bill. Since your tax deductions should increase with home ownership, you probably won't have underwithheld and won't have to pay the IRS in April.

Tip 19.2: For each $2,300 of tax deductibility of your mortgage, you can increase the number of deductions on your W-4 tax withholding form by one. Be aware, however, that if you claim more than ten exemptions, you're likely to incur a visit from the folks at the IRS.

20

See how large a mortgage you can get with your expanded monthly budget for shelter. Take a book of mortgage charts out of the library. For simplicity's sake, turn to the pages that break down thirty-year fixed-rate mortgages at the prevailing interest rate. Look in the monthly payment column to find a payment amount that roughly matches the amount you determined as your monthly affordability. The chart is structured so that you can translate the monthly figure into a gross mortgage amount.

☐ **Done**

21

Figure out how much of a down payment you'll need. Mortgage lenders will generally loan only 80 percent of the purchase price of a home. So if you're able to borrow $100,000, that means you'll be able to buy a $125,000 home . . . if you can come up with the 20 percent—or $25,000— down payment.

☐ **Done**

Tip 21.1: It is possible to put down less cash and borrow greater than 80 percent of the purchase price. But to do so, you must obtain private mortgage insurance (PMI), for which there will be a monthly premium in addition to your mortgage payment.

22

Use savings for your down payment, if you have any. While real estate may no longer be rising in value meteorically, it remains the best vehicle for most Americans to shelter their wealth from taxes, protect themselves from inflation, and save money long term. If you have enough for your down payment in savings, use it—it makes economic sense, and is worth the added quality of life you'll experience.

☐ **Done**

Vacation Home Buyer's Tip 22.1: If you can't afford the down payment for a second property that might remain empty nine months out of the year, consider time shares and fractional interests in quality developments. With a time share, you become one of the owners of a property, with ownership being divided into fifty-two parts, each of which are sold off one or more at a time. Fractional interests are sold in shares and entitle you to use the property a certain number of weeks of the year—for example, a one-tenth share is five weeks. The time is allotted sequentially, so theoretically, you could have a chance to use all the weeks of the year over a four-year period. Floating and fixed time can also be used.

Vacation Home Buyer's Tip 22.2: Consider a lump-sum, long-term lease of your unused time to a friend or relative.

Vacation Home Buyer's Warning 22.3: Time shares can be tough to sell, so be sure your purchase is one sure to increase the quality of your life over a long period of time.

23 If you don't have sufficient savings, start practicing the art of frugality.

Rent videos rather than go to the movies. Cook in rather than eat out. Not only will it help you save money that can go toward your down payment, but it just might awaken in you an appreciation for the pleasures of hearth and home.

☐ **Done**

Tip 23.1: Stop paying for insignificant purchases with credit cards. Save them for big-ticket items, such as furniture, appliances, etc. By doing so, you'll be forcing yourself to be more conscious of where your money is going, and you will think twice about using plastic. The idea is to make purchasing painful.

Tip 23.2: Rather than running to a cash machine every time you need a few bucks, start writing checks instead. Yes, it's more time-consuming, but that's the point. Writing a check and recording where it's going, not to mention deducting it from your balance, is a conscious act, requiring you to stop and really think about where your money is going.

Tip 23.3: Consider selling off collectibles to raise down-payment money. Hold a home-buying party and sell off all the items you don't need.

Tip 23.4: Check out state and local programs for first-time buyers or for low- or moderate-income families. You might be able to get a lower-rate mortgage with a smaller down payment. Information can be obtained by contacting your state or local housing authority, or via any reliable lender or real estate agency.

24

Try saving for a minimum of three months. After three months, you should be able to determine whether or not you'll be able to save or raise sufficient money on your own to pay the down payment. If not, you'll have to borrow it.

☐ **Done**

25

Go back to the nest. Don't be shy about approaching your parents for help with the down payment. Facts are facts: you don't have the economic advantages they did, and they are probably worth three times what you'll ever be. Explain that by helping you out now, they'll be able to share in the joy of your home—something they wouldn't be able to do if they waited until after they were gone to pass your inheritance on to you.

☐ **Done**

Tip 25.1: If your parents seem unwilling or are unable to give you the money gratis, ask if they'll loan it to you. Present it as a bona fide business transaction, asking your folks to become partners in the purchase of your home.

Tip 25.2: If Mom and Dad are still unwilling or unable to help you out, turn to other relatives and friends. Most people are aware that real estate is a sound investment. Present it as such. Take on a silent partner, offering him or her 25 percent ownership of the home while you retain the right to live in it, for example.

When it comes time to sell, the partner (or his or her estate) receives 25 percent of the profit. Consider forming a real estate investment syndicate with five friends, each of whom kicks in capital to purchase the house.

Tip 25.3: Frame all deals made with family and friends according to the degree of risk appropriate to your investor's age and lifestyle. For instance you could offer a guaranteed return, maybe 2 or 3 percent above the cost of living, and have it accrue yearly.

Warning 25.4: Any and all deals should be put in writing, spelling out how the loan will be paid back, and what the lender's exit is. Even the closest relationship may not last forever or stay friendly. That's why it's essential that any financial arrangements be formalized. As far as terms go, I suggest you refrain from offering to pay back the principal over time and instead offer to pay it back out of the proceeds from the sale or a refinancing of the first mortgage.

Tip 25.5: An inducement to a family or friend lender might be a "kicker" in the form of a share of the profits on the ultimate resale.

Vacation Home Buyer's Tip 25.6: Buying a vacation home is a great reason to return to the nest for help. There's an implicit offer of co-enjoyment—parents/grandparents can enjoy the home with you during holidays and the summer—and they'll also have the pleasure of giving their grandchildren their very own "summer camp."

26

Figure out your target. Add your maximum down payment to the amount of mortgage you can afford. Then, add another 20 percent to that figure to afford room for negotiated reductions in price. The resulting number is what you'll give real estate brokers as your target price.

☐ **Done**

27 **Start keeping records.** Begin keeping meticulous records of all the money you spend searching and shopping for a new home. Many of these expenses are deductible from taxable income the year you buy your home.

☐ **Done**

PUTTING YOUR TEAM TOGETHER

typical mistake of home buyers is to venture into the jungle of real estate on their own. Just as you wouldn't take a safari without a guide and a team of support personnel, neither should you try to buy a home on your own. Sure, having a team of professionals on your side can cost money. But it will be more than compensated for by the added protection you'll have from the dangers lurking behind every bush and tree, and even below ground.

28

Begin assembling a team of professionals. While later in the process you'll be using a real estate broker, appraiser, and inspector, at this point your team will consist of an attorney, accountant, insurance broker, and perhaps an architect or designer.

☐ **Done**

29 **Find three candidates for each spot on your roster.** The best way to find candidates is to get recommendations from people in more or less the same financial bracket as you who have gone through the same process. For example, ask friends and co-workers for the names of lawyers they used to buy their homes.

☐ **Done**

Tip 29.1: The professionals you want on your side should have no financial stake in the consummation of your deal. They should charge on an hourly basis or a single flat fee for services rendered. Their advice should be based on what is best for you. (Real estate brokers, who are paid a commission by the seller even though they'll spend most of their time with you, are the exception to the rule.)

Warning 29.2: Avoid professionals who advertise. They've taken out an ad in the Yellow Pages because they need the business.

Warning 29.3: It is not a good idea to use an attorney recommended by a broker.

Tip 29.4: If your friends and co-workers don't provide sufficient candidates, call local professional organizations and ask for recommendations, stressing that you're seeking someone with general real estate expertise.

30

Set up interviews with each potential candidate. Begin by calling each candidate up and making an appointment.

☐ **Done**

Warning 30.1: Some professionals are reluctant to undergo an interview with a potential client. If that is the case, ask for a free consultation. If the pro still balks, scratch him or her off your list.

Warning 30.2: Don't settle for a brief telephone interview, since there's no way of telling over the telephone whether the person will really have your interests at heart.

Tip 30.3: Interviewing your pro in his or her office allows you to see how organized he or she is.

Warning 30.4: If your prospective pro says he or she is too busy to be interviewed, whether it's on the telephone or in person, wave bye-bye and go on to the next name on the list. Anyone who can't give you fifteen minutes is certainly not going to do your bidding when the time comes.

31 Pay attention to the pro's appearance and manners. Your pros should be full-timers, with a fully equipped office and an appearance that inspires confidence.

☐ **Done**

Tip 31.1: Check out the walls of your pro's office. Certificates from established professional associations and commendations from peer groups indicate that he or she is someone who is well respected within the profession.

Warning 31.2: Negative traits in your pro can have a negative effect on your deal. Keep in mind that if the pro does anything during the course of the interview that irritates or annoys you, then it is guaranteed to irritate and annoy others, including the seller and the seller's attorney, broker, and lender.

Tip 31.3: Look for someone who makes eye contact when you speak, listens to what you say, and expresses interest in your individual situation.

Warning 31.4: If the pro takes telephone calls during your interview, think twice about whether you want him or her on your team. Why? Because he or she will have no qualms about doing the same thing when you're at your wit's end waiting for a response to an urgent inquiry.

32

Be an inquiring interviewer. The secret question in any conversation with a professional is "why?"—not "how?" Any pro who isn't willing to discuss why he or she does something isn't likely to put his or her heart into working for you. Ask why a certain procedure takes a specified amount of time, or why the pro's fee is the stated amount.

☐ **Done**

Tip 32.1: Ask about the professional's commitment to ongoing education. It's crucial that he or she is up-to-date with current technological and industry developments.

Tip 32.2: Don't be put off by the pro who says he or she doesn't know the answer to a question but will find it out. This shows honesty and a willingness to work with you—which is exactly what you want.

Tip 32.3: Listen carefully to the pro's answers to your questions. Are they well thought out, or do they sound as if they're coming from a script that has been used hundreds of times before? Does he or she offer options, or do you get the feeling it's "my way or the highway"? Are you confident this person would be able to get your point across during negotiations?

Warning 32.4: If at any point you suspect or discover a candidate has lied about anything, leave. The same holds true for any professionals who say that if they had to, they would lie for you.

Tip 32.5: Find out how long candidates have been in their field and what percentage of their business involves residential real estate. Ask how many transactions the candidate has been involved with in the area you've settled on. Try to get specific answers. Pros learn by doing. Quaint as it may sound, age and experience not only count but are downright essential.

33

Ask about and negotiate the fee. Find out what his or her fee is, and negotiate accordingly. Chances are he or she might offer to reduce the fee by eliminating some services. Try to get a ceiling on hours and a commitment from the pro to keep the hours lean.

☐ **Done**

Warning 33.1: Never criticize a pro's fee as too high, or say the services aren't worth it. That's an attack on the person, not the services.

Warning 33.2: Never set a fee based on the consideration (i.e., 1 percent of the purchase price). You are entitled to the best no matter what the size of the deal (the same hours are involved, whether you're talking about $100,000 or $1,000,000).

34

Get references. Before leaving the office, get the names and numbers of the candidate's last three home-buying clients (they are less likely to be rigged), and then call to talk with them. Press for factual responses to your questions rather than opinions.

☐ **Done**

Tip 34.1: When checking up on an attorney's references, ask how long it took for calls to be returned, as well as the length of time the contract negotiation took and whether or not the attorney was present at the closing.

Tip 34.2: In the case of an accountant, find out how much experience he or she has had reviewing the prospectuses of co-ops or condos. Make sure he or she knows the most important elements of the building financials.

35

Look for an attorney who's capable of donning many hats. He or she will need to be an expert negotiator, financial adviser, contract reader, and closing supervisor.

☐ **Done**

Tip 35.1: I suggest you steer clear of large law firms. The reason? You want a personal relationship with your attorney, which is very difficult to achieve if you go with a large firm. Large firms see nothing wrong with sending associates and paralegals to closings. You want someone who will be with you every step of the way, from house hunting to closing.

Warning 35.2: Brokers who tell you that real estate transactions don't require an attorney are dead wrong. Despite the fact that many states now utilize forms allowing the broker to handle the funds and negotiations, it's in your interest to have a legal adviser looking on. Never sign anything without speaking to your lawyer first. This also applies to states where the title company handles all the arrangements.

Tip 35.3: Real estate attorneys usually bill on an hourly basis. Arrange to have yours bill you regularly (monthly or weekly, whichever you prefer) so you can keep track of fees. Be sure to find out whether you'll be billed for telephone calls and paralegal services. Press for associates' time to be billed at a lower rate than the attorney's. Be prepared for your attorney to bill you for between four to six hours (assuming competence on the seller's side).

Tip 35.4: Don't worry if the broker mutters that your attorney is an obstacle. While you don't want your attorney to be unreasonable, you do want him or her to have your best interests at heart and to raise objections and concerns along the way.

Retirement Home Buyer's Tip 35.5: Professional legal advice is an absolute must for retirement-home buyers. You are possibly investing a sizable portion of your personal financial resources and, as a retiree, you have little chance to recoup from mistakes. Make sure your attorney is

someone who has experience with the purchase of homes in adult communities.

Retirement Home Buyer'sTip 35.6: If you are buying out of state, be sure to use a local representative.

Retirement Home Buyer's Warning 35.7: If required, be sure to check state files regarding the formal status of the community: Is it a skilled nursing facility, intermediate care facility, or adult home as well as a retirement community?

36 **Make sure your accountant is a CPA.** This is an assurance of accountability (no pun intended). Insist that he or she be the one who will be handling your business personally. If any work will be delegated to staff members, ask about their fees and qualifications.

☐ **Done**

Tip 36.1: Make sure your accountant has some knowledge of real estate.

Tip 36.2: As with your attorney, your accountant will charge on an hourly basis. Obtain a budget and request to be billed periodically.

Apartment Buyer's Tip 36.3: An accountant is essential in the purchase of a co-op or condo. A good one will be able to guesstimate future maintenance costs and examine the financial structure of the corporation in under one and a half hours. He or she should also be able to predict and prepare for all the tax implications of a real estate purchase.

37 Go with a local insurance broker as opposed to an insurance agent. Brokers are independent operators who should serve their clients' interests, not that of a particular insurance company. Local brokers will be aware of specific area ordinances that could affect your coverage.

☐ **Done**

Tip 37.1: Ask the insurance broker about contacts he or she has made with various insurance companies so you can gauge his or her ability to help settle claims.

Warning 37.2: Never buy insurance over-the-counter in a retail store.

Warning 37.3: You want nuts-and-bolts coverage from a company with a rep-utation for service. Avoid vanity riders, e.g., being put up in the best hotel if your house is destroyed.

38

Hire your architect now if you know you'll be needing construction work done. Homes that will need to be expanded or converted for special needs should be examined by an architect before they are purchased. Call the American Institute of Architects to get the names of those in your area in good standing.

☐ **Done**

Tip 38.1: When interviewing a prospective architect, ask to see plans and drawings of homes he or she has done in the recent past. Don't be shy about expressing your likes and dislikes.

Tip 38.2: More than with other members of your team, a good personal rapport with an architect is essential. His or her personality should be a close match with yours, at least where taste and style are concerned.

Tip 38.3: Architects' fees and responsibilities are spelled out in a written contract that includes details of the services to be provided. Architects charge on an hourly basis or establish their fee as a percentage of construction costs. Your attorney should play an active role in negotiating this contract.

Warning 38.4: Be aware that most architects lack management experience when it comes to overseeing the job site (otherwise known as your home).

Warning 38.5: Since architects are fond of using materials they see in design magazines, make sure yours confines him- or herself to local products. Your Utah home doesn't need Vermont marble.

Warning 38.6: Tempting as it may be, avoid hiring a relative to do architectural work. This is not the time to give your nephew his first shot at design fame.

DO A LOCATION ANALYSIS

With your goals and financial resources established, and your professional team in place, you're ready to start looking for a place to live. That doesn't mean looking at individual houses . . . at least not yet. It means analyzing locations or areas—whether cities, villages, towns, counties, or the individual neighborhoods or enclaves within them—to determine which are right for you and your family.

39

Do a location analysis. Before you even begin looking at specific houses, walk—or drive—yourself around the area you think you might be interested in living in. Think of it as a learning experience. Scout during both day and night to see if there are any dramatic changes when the sun goes down. By the time you've scoured your location for a week, you'll not only be knowledgeable about the area but you'll be an educated home consumer.

☐ **Done**

40

Start by looking at residential areas. Observe, observe, observe. Are the houses and lawns well maintained? Are the streets heavily traveled or are cars rare? Are there streetlights? Remember: a well-cared-for town indicates a healthy community.

☐ **Done**

41

Next look at commercial areas.
Pay close attention to the business district, noting how many stores—and what type—are opening. Gourmet coffee shops indicate the neighborhood is going upscale. Furniture and appliance rental businesses indicate the reverse. Lots of vacant store fronts for rent indicate economic trouble has already hit.

☐ **Done**

Tip 41.1: Don't forget to take into account your own shopping needs while on your analysis tour. Check out supermarkets, drugstores, etc. If these stores are clean and bustling, chances are this part of town is on the upward slope.

Warning 41.2: Stores with yellowing window displays or dusty shelves indicate that the business, if not that entire part of town, is on the downward slope.

Tip 41.3: Pay close attention to store hours. Those in healthy towns or neighborhoods have long hours and tend to remain open even on Sundays.

42

Explore the community's cultural and recreational facilities. Healthy communities also tend to be culturally enlightened, with ample recreational facilities. Scope out whether the community you want to buy in has movie theaters, museums, and parks.

☐ **Done**

Tip 42.1: Check to see what the recreation facilities of the town are actually like. Are the parks well populated and pleasant? Or are they littered with beer cans and inhabited by unsavory characters?

43 **Investigate the local government.** Look for a full-time, professional government. A good way to see if the one in your prospective town is any good is by calling the state government, which probably rates its municipalities.

☐ **Done**

Tip 43.1: Check out the attitude of the local government toward services. Full-time professional police and fire departments are good signs. Find out whether you'll have to pay for garbage collection; whether water is included in your property tax bill, or if it is billed separately; and whether there are municipal sewers. The city or county clerk's office or the editor of the local newspaper can provide you with this information.

Tip 43.2: Call the tax assessor's office and find out the assessment tax rate of the community and if increases are planned. Any community in the process of reassessment is guaranteed to be in for a tax hike, since no municipality looks to cut its revenues.

Tip 43.3: Call your stockbroker and find out what the Moody's investment rating is for the municipality. If the community's bonds aren't A-rated, think twice about relocating there.

44

If you are house hunting in a small town, contact the local banker and arrange to see him or her. The banker, eager for your future business, will likely go out of his or her way to be helpful. Pump him or her for info on the town's government, as well as the name of the best broker in town. Make sure you ask about the town's economic health, real estate market, the tax base, and whether or not taxes are on the way up or down. Don't neglect to ask about the most expensive part of town and how long it takes homes there to sell, as well as how far apart the asking and selling prices are.

☐ **Done**

Tip 44.1: Try to be as specific as possible when gleaning information. "Are there any good restaurants in town?" lends itself to a vague and totally subjective answer. On the other hand, asking if there are any good Chinese restaurants in town will result in specifics, and will probably lead to further conversation.

Tip 44.2: Find out what is the economic base of the community. It's crucial that the area have a sound commercial or industrial foundation, otherwise homeowners are the ones who wind up footing the lion's share of the tax bill for services. The more diversified the economic base the better, since diversity tends to ensure stability.

Tip 44.3: Try to get some hard demographic info on the residents of the area, such as age, family size, average income, level of education, and socioeconomic status.

45 Research the area's climate.

Weather and climate can strongly affect property values. Make sure you know what both are like by checking local papers and talking to insurance agents. You'll need to know if the area is at risk for a flood, as well as what the annual rainfall and snowfall numbers are, and temperature highs and lows. Keep on the lookout for any environmental problems specific to the area.

☐ **Done**

46

If your children are of school age, check out the school system. The best communities tend to have the best teachers. The educational values of the community will become apparent when you find out what the student/teacher ratio is and how much money the district spends per student. Find out what special programs and courses are offered, and check to see where the school district spends its money. If you can, sit in on a class so you can observe the quality of education firsthand.

☐ **Done**

Tip 46.1: See if there is a public library in the area. Towns without one aren't too concerned about the education of their children.

47

Pick up copies of the local newspaper. Go straight for the real estate and want ads. Since many towns have more than one paper, seek out the one that features the police blotter—this is a sure indication that the paper isn't biased in any way toward local law enforcement and government.

☐ **Done**

48

Don't be afraid to scratch the surface of what you see. Call the local utilities, chamber of commerce, and the regional tourist bureau and ask for information they have on the area. The info might be biased, but you're smart enough to glean the facts from the hype.

☐ **Done**

Tip 48.1: Pop in on the local power, utility, and telephone companies. They'll be able to provide you with data on future energy users as well as projections on longterm energy growth or shrinkage. They will also give you an idea about industrial and commercial growth in the area.

Tip 48.2: If you have time, pay a visit to the local planning or building department so you can see what is planned for the future. Check to see if the town or city has a master plan. If it doesn't, that bodes poorly: developers are free to do what they want. Or, it could mean that the town has grown as much as it's going to. Check state and local departments of works for plans to widen roads or make other improvements. Today's intimate, winding access can be tomorrow's main thoroughfare.

Tip 48.3: Pay close attention to the zoning and land-use plans of the community. In an urban area, that means the block and surrounding two or three blocks on all sides. In suburbia, it means the entire town or village. Check for vacant lots or buildings about to be demolished. If a home you're interested in has windows overlooking an empty lot, assume it won't be empty for long, and the worst imaginable structure—a maximum-security prison, for instance—will be built there.

49

If you're a retiree, rent before you buy. If you're an older American shopping for a retirement home in which you hope to spend the rest of your life, consider renting in the area before buying. It's the only way you'll be able to see if it's really the right place for you.

☐ **Done**

50

If you're buying a vacation home, rent before you buy. Don't buy anywhere you haven't vacationed several times. More important, never buy a home on a first visit to a time-share resort or new resort community.

☐ **Done**

Vacation Home Buyer's Tip 50.1: While vacationing in an area, study the real estate market using actual sales prices, not advertised asking prices. Look at time shares for sale, and talk to leading real estate brokers in the community. If you're planning to rent the property out, make sure there's a firm in town that will be able to manage the property while you're away.

Vacation Home Buyer's Tip 50.2: If you absolutely need the rental income to afford your purchase of a vacation home, then your best bet is a popular resort area with one or two long rental seasons, i.e., one that features skiing in the winter and camping in the summer.

Vacation Home Buyer's Tip 50.3: If your primary motivation for buying a vacation home is solely for the enjoyment of your family, the best areas to investigate are waterfront property; apartments or townhouses in cities that are hubs of international travel and culture; and rural acreage near expanding metropolitan areas.

Tip 50.4: Location, location, location.

FINDING A BROKER AND HOUSE HUNTING

There's a great deal of confusion about real estate brokers. They work with buyers, but get paid by sellers. At best, they work for the deal, since they only get a commission when a home is actually sold. Despite all the confusion, they remain, I believe, an essential part of the house-hunting process. Without them, you'd have to give up your full-time job and spend all your days and nights house hunting. And brokerage is nearly always built into the purchase price whether you use a broker or not.

51

Resolve to work with one reliable broker. After more than thirty-five years in the industry, I've come to the conclusion that it's in a buyer's best interests to find one good broker and stick with him or her throughout the hunt.

☐ **Done**

Tip 51.1: Look for a real estate broker as soon as you have completed your location analysis. He or she should be a member of the National Association of Realtors and should specialize in the area in which you are interested. Look for one who is part of a multiple listing service—that's a group of area brokers who share information on all the local properties up for sale. Using a broker who's part of a multiple listing service will improve your chances of seeing a wide variety of available homes. Ask your professionals for recommendations.

Warning 51.2: Avoid homes with "for sale by owner" signs on the front lawn or advertised directly by the owner. Chances are high the sellers of such homes have no clue about the value of the property or the delicate dance that is the selling process. A home sold without a broker will not save anyone money, since the seller thinks he or she can boost the price by the 6 percent not being spent on a commission and you'll think you can cut your offer by the same 6 percent. While it might be tempting to see what such owner-offered homes have to offer inside, save yourself some aspirin and don't bother.

Tip 51.3: Try to pick one top candidate from among the recommended brokers. Make your choice according to another pro's high praise or the broker's visibility in the market. Don't worry about making a mistake. After one trip with a broker, you'll be able to tell if he or she is right for you.

52 **Set up an appointment with your top candidate.** Arrive prepared to judge not only homes but the broker as well. Do not bring the whole family with you—kids can get cranky mighty fast and will only distract you.

☐ **Done**

Tip 52.1: Dress conservatively and neatly. You want people to know you mean business.

Tip 52.2: Bring the following items with you on your hunt: an instant camera with film; a small tape recorder; a tape measure; a compass; pencils and notepad; binoculars; and your list of needs, wants, and priorities . . . and a tennis ball.

53

Engage in a dialogue with the broker. Tell the broker your needs and wants. Probe for his knowledge of the community; ask where she lives, where the kids go to school, etc. Be sure to find out how long the broker has been in business. If he or she is new or is doing it part-time, find another broker. You want someone with experience, who can devote full time and attention to your needs.

☐ **Done**

Tip 53.1: Pay close attention to the questions the broker asks you. They should be extensive, indicating he or she is interested in gleaning your home-buying priorities.

Tip 53.2: Make sure your broker prescreens the homes before taking you to see them.

Warning 53.3: If a broker advises you to bypass professionals or tries to steer you toward professionals who "won't screw up the deal," don't listen. Such brokers only have their own interests at heart, and will feel no guilt over hooking you up with questionable professionals if it means they'll clinch the deal.

Warning 53.4: Sadly, discrimination can and does still occur in the real estate market. If you're disabled, a person of color, a religious or ethnic minority, were born in another country, or are gay, and a broker says you "wouldn't feel comfortable" in a certain neighborhood, you're being discriminated against and need to take action. Start by confronting the person and demanding an explanation. If the explanation is insufficient and/or the discrimination continues, write a letter about the broker to his or her employer and send a copy to the Board of Realtors. It goes without saying that you should find another broker as well.

Tip 53.5: You can test your broker's mettle by giving him or her a copy of your game plan and then going on a site visit. If the homes he or she takes you to see come close to what you're looking for, you've got a good broker. If he or she takes you to see homes that are a far cry from your needs and wants, wave *hasta la vista* and start looking for another broker. The sooner you hook up with a broker who can envision your dream as clearly as you, the sooner you'll find the home you're looking for.

54

Let the broker chauffeur you around, and not vice versa. This will free you up to take notes, gauge traffic, and observe the general area, noting specifics about the block and neighborhood. If you see a major factory complex nearby or a garbage dump or sewer plant, don't even get out of the car. Not only are environmental problems bad for animals, children, and other living things, but they can destroy the resale value of a home.

☐ **Done**

Tip 54.1: On your way to the first home, ask the broker: how long it has been on the market; when it was built and when any extensions were done; if the brokerage firm helped set the price; the personality of the seller; age of the children; evidence of sickness; why the home is being sold (job relocation? retirement? divorce?); why prior deals, if any, fell apart; and what offers, if any, have been rejected. Get the broker to provide the information you need to make a sound judgment.

Tip 54.2: The broker will always take the most scenic road to view an offering. Ask to take the shortcut on the way back.

Tip 54.3: Don't see more than five homes a day. This will keep you from confusing them later that evening when the time comes to go over what you've seen and compare notes. Ask the broker if he or she can schedule visits to houses near to each other so you waste no time in traffic. Start early so you see all homes in the clear light of day.

Tip 54.4: Each house tour should take half an hour, max. This gives you enough time to decide if the home fits in with your needs and wants and is a sound invest-ment.

55

Begin by examining the exterior of the house. Check out the roof, chimney, exterior walls, and foundation.

☐ **Done**

Tip 55.1: Check out the roof, using your binoculars, to see if there are any sags or dips that could indicate a structural problem. Note what kind of material is used: tile, slate, wood, or asphalt. Is the roof flat or pitched? Does it look as if it's in good shape, or are there gaps in the roofing material? Does it appear to have been repaired lately?

Tip 55.2: Examine the chimney, flashing, leaders, and gutters. Are water stains visible? Are there enough down spouts? Check the ground near the down spouts for signs of flooding. Does it look as if the gutters have been cleaned recently?

Tip 55.3: Note what the exterior walls are constructed of and covered with: masonry, clapboard, wooden shingles, or aluminum siding. What condition is the wall covering in? Do shingles need to be replaced? Is paint blistering? Is there any evidence of dry rot or decay, such as crumbling windowsills or doorjambs?

Warning 55.4: If you spot any zigzag cracking in the masonry or walls, or if there are any signs of uneven settling, go no further. While hairline cracks in masonry are common in older homes, any signs of recent damage that look as though they've been covered up should give you pause. If anything looks suspicious, take a photo with your instant camera.

Tip 55.5: Note the number and type of windows on each side of the house. Are the window frames in good shape, or are they rotting? Does each window have a storm and screen? Make sure all windowpanes are in place. Cracked glass indicates the owner's approach to maintenance is "relaxed," to put it politely.

Tip 55.6: Keep your eyes peeled for signs of insect infestation, paying special attention to whether there are undue concen- trations of insects at the joints between foundation and sid- ing, roof and wall, and window and wall.

Tip 55.7: The key aes- thetic question to ask yourself when exam- ining the outside of a home is: Does it fit in with the homes of the neighbors? Remem- ber: one day you may be selling this home.

Tip 55.8: Take at least one full frame picture of the front of the home so you can use it to jog your memory later on.

56

Peruse the deck, patio, and porch if the house has any of these features. Do they appear sound, or are they in disrepair? Are they in keeping with the style of the home, or do they look as if Uncle Gino built them on his day off?

☐ **Done**

Warning 56.1: A poorly built and maintained wooden addition that has begun to rot or decay can spread its sickness to the rest of the house. And if the structure isn't sound, it could be placing stress on the rest of the house.

57

Don't forget about security. How close are the neighbors? Can rear windows be reached from the ground? Check to see if doors and windows lock and if there's an alarm system in place.

☐ **Done**

58

Explore the yard. Pay close attention to the lawn, trees, and shrubs. Are they well maintained? Check out the fences and the sheds, noting whether they're in good shape or falling apart. Look to see if the driveway is paved, what condition the sidewalk is in, and whether there are any streetlights. If they're interesting, take photos of the front, rear, and side landscaping. Jot down any landscaping problems that might need attention.

☐ **Done**

Tip 58.1: Check out the views surrounding the home, making sure not to take anybody's word about "obscured views."

Warning 58.2: Any site that doesn't allow water to drain off it is in danger of flooding. Make sure you check out the grading of the property and the surrounding area, ascertaining whether the house is at the bottom of or alongside a hill.

59

Draw a simple map of the site. Sketch the layout of the house on the lot, placing windows in their proper areas. Using the compass, note exposures for each side of the house, and check what types of landscaping are near or around the exposures. Southern exposures should be protected by deciduous trees—ones that drop their leaves in winter. Northern exposures should have evergreens nearby, offering protection in winter. This information will also help you determine which rooms get morning light, which afternoon light, and which will be forever dark.

☐ **Done**

60

If you're still interested, move inside. If you're not interested, leave now. If you are, cross the threshold into the house, paying close attention to the entryway. A good entryway should shield you from the elements and feature wide steps or a wide walk.

☐ **Done**

Tip 60.1: Once inside, your general goal should be to think about the flow of rooms and the traffic patterns your family will make through them. As you move from room to room, sketch the floor plan, indicating doors and windows. Be sure to note if there are rooms that can only be entered by going through another room, or rooms that have two entryways.

Tip 60.2: As you tour the home, make special note of the walls, floors, and ceilings throughout. While it's not uncommon for old houses to "settle," causing the floor to be slightly uneven, this should not be the case in a new home. If a tennis ball rolls on the floor of a new home, you've got a problem. Check to see if the walls are in good shape. Are there holes and cracks? What about the molding—is any missing? Check the ceiling for signs of water damage. If you spot a stain, look down to the corresponding area on the floor. Determine each room's approximate size as you move through it by using your tape measure. Try to get a sense, or feeling, from the house.

Tip 60.3: Try to determine the seller's personality as best you can. Check out the decor of the house and the condition of the yard. See what kind of magazines are lying around, and check out the family photos. Any info you gather can work to your advantage when you're sitting across the bargaining table from this person.

Warning 60.4: Electrical service can be a source of concern, especially in apartments or older homes. Check to see whether the outlets are modern or old-fashioned. If outlets accept three-prong, grounded plugs, that's good. If the house seems filled with extension cords and plug adapters, assume you'll have to upgrade electrical service upon moving in (which can be expensive).

Apartment Buyer's Tip 60.5: Views from apartments often carry more weight than those from a single-family home, since apartments by their nature are smaller. Other important features to study when apartment hunting are the downstairs lobby, hallways, laundry rooms, trash-disposal areas, elevator interiors, and basement facilities. The condition of these areas will give you a good idea whether the co-op or condo you're considering is well maintained or not.

61

Start in the kitchen. Since the kitchen is the most important room in the house, check it out first.

☐ **Done**

Tip 61.1: Make sure you note the following when in the kitchen: whether there is room to eat; the amount of counter space; whether the major work areas—sink, stove, refrigerator—are set up in a triangular relationship to each other; the condition of the appliances; and whether there is a window over the sink. If the kitchen needs to be redone and you can't afford it, don't even think about buying this home—kitchen renovations are ranked number one in terms of cost.

62 **Move on to the dining room.** Check to see if it has adequate access to both the kitchen and the living room. Is it large enough to accommodate at least six to eight people around the table?

☐ **Done**

Warning 62.1:
Beware of strategically placed mirrors in hallways that could be used to give the false illusion of space.

Tip 62.2: When you enter a room, turn off the lights. This will give you a real idea of how much natural light the room gets.

63

Move on to the living room. Pay close attention to the size of the room, especially if the house has no den. You want it to be large enough to accommodate the family and guests. If there is a den, you can probably get by with a smaller living room.

☐ **Done**

Warning 63.1: Since rugs can be useful in hiding damage to the floor, make sure you lift small, unusually placed ones up to check beneath. Remember that any fixture or furnishing that seems odd could be there to mask a problem.

64

Move on to the family room. If there's a family room or den, note how large it is. If it's going to be the place where entertainment, informal dining, and family activities are held, you want to make sure it will hold all the furniture you'll need.

☐ **Done**

65 **Move on to the bedrooms.** When checking each bedroom, note how much light is coming into the room and how close each bedroom is to the bathroom. Determine whether the bedroom will be large enough for each probable occupant.

☐ **Done**

Tip 65.1: Don't forget about closets. Older homes that haven't been updated may not have one in every bedroom.

Warning 65.2: If the main building doesn't provide you with enough storage space for your needs, don't count on an outbuilding or garage to make up the difference.

66 **Move on to the bathroom(s).** All bathrooms should have either windows or working ventilation systems. Check to see if the bathroom has a walk-in shower or a bath/shower combination. Turn on each faucet in the bathroom and check for water pressure. Note the number of electrical outlets, as well as the condition of the tiles and the walls. Inspect the fixtures and check the drainage in the tub, toilet, and sink. Drop a wad of toilet paper into the bowl and see how quickly the tank flushes.

☐ **Done**

Warning 66.1: Never assume you can add another bathroom to bring the home up to your standards. The cost can be prohibitive. Any home in which more than one person lives should have at least two toilets.

67 **Explore the attic.** Are there permanent attic stairs, or pull-down stairs in the hallway? Is access limited to a hatch in the closet?

☐ **Done**

68

Move down to the basement. Some things to keep in mind if there is a basement: Is it well-lit? Does it smell of mildew? Are there signs of water damage? Do you have to enter from the outside, or is there inside access? If there is no basement, where are the furnace, water heater, and laundry facilities located?

☐ **Done**

Warning: 68.1: If the basement has a sump pump or dehumidifier, ask why. Chances are they're there because of previous flooding. Keep in mind that basements that have suffered water damage are easily camouflaged with paint and a dehumidifier.

Tip 68.2: Make sure the house has adequate laundry facilities. A washer/dryer setup in the basement may not be aesthetically pleasing, but it beats hauling your wash to the Laundromat.

Tip 68.3: Make sure to check the electrical service while in the basement. If fuses rather than circuit breakers are installed, the service is the same as the original construction. Fuses covered in silver foil or pennies used to replace fuses are not only fire hazards but are signs of inadequate service. Keep in mind that modern circuit-breaker panels are a plus, especially if they're labeled and allow for more lines to be added. A 100-amp service is adequate for most families.

69

While exploring the basement, find out how old the home is, what systems—if any—have been replaced, and when. All parts of a home have a life expectancy and will need to be replaced at some time. By finding out the age of the house as well as that of the systems involved, you'll be able to estimate future costs and expenses. Remember that deferred maintenance is never a money saver. In fact, it breeds additional costs—you end up paying more if you buy a less expensive home and have to fix a systems problem than if you buy a slightly more expensive home with modern systems.

☐ **Done**

Tip 69.1: After five years, expect to replace or repair: exterior paint on wood or brick; interior paint on doors, walls, and trim; wallpaper; lightbulbs; and gravel walks.

Tip 69.2: Between five and ten years, you'll be forking over bucks for: screen doors; carpeting; splash blocks; asphalt driveways; and possibly new appliances such as washers, dryers, humidifiers, and dishwashers.

Tip 69.3: Once ten to fifteen years have passed, some serious maintenance problems may occur. Look for problems in: tar/gravel roofs; storm doors; precast decks and porches; interior doors; exterior wood trim; painted aluminum siding; vinyl floorings; kitchen and bath exhaust fans; gas water heaters; airconditioner compressors; sprinkler systems; and concrete walks.

Tip 69.4: As a home closes its second decade you might have to pay for: asphalt shingles; kitchen cabinets and bathroom vanities; countertops; tub enclosures and shower doors; electric ranges, ovens, and refrigerators; steel and china sinks; flush valves; and septic systems.

Tip 69.5: When a home is between twenty and thirty years old, you might need to update: circuit breakers; ceiling and baseboard heating fixtures; fences and screens; wood and metal shutters; garage doors; and asphalt roofs.

Tip 69.6: Between thirty and fifty years, be prepared to invest in: new circuit-breaker panels; galvanized iron or plastic pipes; heating and ventilation ducts; wood, tile, and asbestos roofs; casement, double-hung, and jalousie windows; interior stairways; drywall and interior wood trim; and flagstone floors.

Tip 69.7: As a home approaches fifty years old, all remaining original systems will have to be replaced.

70

Once you've completed the tour, ask the broker for comparables. Comparables are the actual sale prices of homes similar to the one you've just seen, not the asking price. The more recent the comp and closer to the home in question, the more valid it is.

☐ **Done**

Warning 70.1: If the broker tries to pressure you by saying that someone else is ready to buy the house, tell him or her you hope the other family will be happy there, and leave. Good brokers don't pressure. Auctions are deadly.

71 **After one day, make a judgment of your broker.** If he or she has shown you homes that generally match your needs and wants, has been helpful and knowledgeable, and appears to be ethical, stick with him or her. If you aren't happy, go back to step 51.

☐ **Done**

72

Go home and study your notes. Go over all the information you've gathered and decide if any of the homes you've seen interest you enough to place an offer. If none do, call the broker the next morning, schedule another appointment, and go back to step 54. If you've decided to place an offer, move on to Stage 5.

☐ **Done**

NEGOTIATING THE SELLING PRICE

Now begins the delicate dance of negotiation. Your aim should be a "fair" price. To get there you need to approach the process honestly in an effort to strike a deal that will satisfy both parties' needs. How to do this? By gathering together all the information you've gleaned from the broker, plus your location and site analyses, and making an offer that reflects the true market value of the house—not the inflated price the seller thinks he's entitled to or the lowball figure you think you can get away with. Remember: you're negotiating a deal, not a "win."

73

Realize that the fair market value of the house is a range, not a single price. Real estate is not an exact science. Therefore, the value of homes falls in a range of around 15 percent up and down—$85,000 to $115,000, for instance. Sellers want a price at the top of the range, while buyers want a price at the bottom.

☐ **Done**

74

Determine the fair market value range of the home. The best way to do this is to factor together actual comparables (those based on sales) and the asking price of comparable homes currently on the market. Also factor in the appraised value if you have an appraisal done.

☐ **Done**

75

Look at relevant comparables.
Go back to the comps the broker gave you. If they don't seem valid—perhaps they aren't as similar and/or as recent as you'd like—ask for more.

☐ **Done**

76 **Hire an appraiser.** I've become an advocate of getting appraisals on all homes selling for more than $350,000. The cost—$150 to $350—is well worth what you get: the most exact possible estimate of value.

☐ **Done**

Tip 76.1: Ask your lawyer for the names of appraisers in the area. Look for one with experience who's a member of either the Society of Real Estate Appraisers or the American Institute of Real Estate Appraisers. He or she should specialize in residential real estate.

Tip 76.2: Ask the appraiser if he or she has done any work in the neighborhood in question. Find out how many appraisals he or she has done there in the past year, and ask to see a sample of a recent one.

Tip 76.3: Give the appraiser the exact location of the home in question, as well as the details on the size of the house, number of bedrooms and bathrooms, and any other details affecting value. The appraiser will most likely consult records and find the three most recent comps in the area. He or she may also visit the home in question to determine whether it's worth more or less than the selling price of the three comp sales.

77 Find out the seller's motivation.

Once you've got an inkling of what the fair market value of the house is, try to find out why the house is up for sale. Does the seller have a deadline looming over his head? Is he or she moving to a smaller home because the nest is empty? Or is he or she buying up because of an increased income? Would the seller consider assisting you in the purchase by taking back a second trust? All this info can be gleaned by asking the broker.

☐ **Done**

Tip 77.1: Obviously, the more pressure a seller is under, the more likely he or she is to settle for a price at the bottom end of the fair market value range.

78

Come up with your "bottom line." Based on the comps and the appraisal, come up with a figure you feel is "top dollar" above which you won't pay.

☐ **Done**

Tip 78.1: Keep this figure uppermost in your mind and stick to it. You've already stretched as far as you can go. Don't allow the broker to pressure you, purring that this is the only house for you. Rationally, you know it isn't. You need only open the telephone book to see there are lots of other brokers out there. Tell this one to take a hike if he or she pulls any of those stunts.

Warning 78.2: Never reveal your bottom line to the seller or the broker and never, ever stretch beyond it.

79

Come up with an initial offer. In formulating your initial offer, keep in mind the figures given you by the appraiser, and set your counteroffer below the low end of the appraised range. Do this even if the seller's price is within the market value range. Your objective is to give both sides an opportunity to move toward fair market value, but to end up at a price in the low end of the range.

☐ **Done**

Warning 79.1: *Never* meet the price offered by the seller, even if your analysis shows it's below the appraised judgment. This would preclude a fair negotiation, since the seller has set the price at a higher level than he or she is willing to accept. By meeting it, you're ensuring the seller won't have to move at all and may be prompting him or her to pull the home off the market and reprice it. Remember: a negotiation is fair only if it requires both sides to move.

Warning 79.2: Do not enter into negotiations for the purchase of any home that has a market range more than 20 percent above your affordability figure. It doesn't matter that you love the house to death; you've got to be able to afford it. Try to keep your emotions in check while never forgetting what your affordability is.

Tip 79.3: Feel free to accept advice from attorneys, appraisers, even brokers, but never forget that you're the one in control.

Warning 79.4: Some homes have been so overpriced that your initial offer could be construed as insulting. Ask the broker to communicate to the seller that you're inclined to make an offer, but the seller might want to reconsider the asking price first.

Tip 79.5: In an active market, a seller will sit tight if you give notice (five to seven days) that you'll be making an offer.

Tip 79.6: Have your bank prequalify you for a mortgage. This makes you appear to be an all-cash buyer.

80

Submit your offer. Convey your offer through the real estate broker. He or she will report back to you on the seller's feelings.

☐ **Done**

Tip 80.1 : Always supply a reason for your offer. If you've found defects in the home, point them out . . . gently. Tell the broker about your appraisal. Mention the work you anticipate you'll have to do in the house, whether it's a new paint job or remodeling the kitchen. Place the onus on your wants and needs, rather than saying the house is too small or the price too high. This safeguards against the owner's becoming defensive.

Tip 80.2: Remember that brokers are bound by a code of ethics and must convey all offers to the seller. If a broker says an offer is too low, tell him or her to convey it anyway, along with your reasons. If you discover a broker has at any time lied to you, bypass him or her if you can. You don't want a deal to fall apart because of a broker.

81 **Study counteroffers carefully.** In most cases, sellers respond to an initial offer with a counteroffer that indicates they'll accept a final price that's midpoint between your first number and their first counter.

☐ **Done**

Tip 81.1: Don't get upset if there's no response to your offer. Indicate that you're willing to negotiate and, if you have to, provide a list of significant problems with the property to the seller, including what it will cost you to repair them. Toss in a copy of the appraisal for good measure. If the seller is astute, he or she will respond. If not, you're probably dealing with someone whose grip on real estate reality is tenuous at best. Some sellers put their homes on the market at a "dream" price, and then refuse to budge. Tell the broker to ask the seller if this refusal to move indicates an unwillingness to negotiate. If this query elicits no response, drop the matter, telling the broker you'll only be interested when and if the process is open to negotiation. That puts the ball firmly in the seller's court.

82

Engage in incremental negotiating. Offering yet more factual data or, reiterating your original reasons, respond to the seller's first counter with an incremental increase in your offer. If the seller makes frequent, small concessions in price, respond in kind. If the seller makes major concessions, respond with major concessions of your own. This could indicate the seller is eager to close the deal quickly, which can work to your advantage.

☐ **Done**

Warning 82.1: Never bid against yourself. If you fail to get a response to an offer, ask if the last counter-offer was the seller's final price. Generally, the smaller the concessions get, the closer you are to both parties' bottom lines. But never follow up your own offer with another. If you have to, break a deadlock by stating the obvious: you're willing to raise your price if the seller is willing to lower his or hers. Simple though this may be, it has been known to save the day.

Warning 82.2: If you find you're competing with another buyer, get out of the process. You want to be the only one making an offer. Ask that you be contacted once the negotiations with the other buyer are completed.

Tip 82.3: Always be prepared to walk away from a deal. Remember that there's no such thing as a home you can't live without. The time to fall in love with a dwelling is after you own it, not before.

83

Don't give up if you reach an impasse. Instead, tell the broker you need his or her help. Suggest that all parties work together and make sacrifices to reach an agreement. The longer the negotiation drags on, the more likely it is the broker will push the seller to cut a deal, even cutting his or her commission if necessary.

☐ **Done**

Tip 83.1: Another way of surmounting an impasse is by introducing new elements into the deal, such as creative financing. Ask the seller to finance the deal in exchange for accepting the most recent offer. He or she can "take back" a mortgage at a rate that's 1 to 2 percent below that of another lender. Offer to tailor a mortgage to the seller's financial needs, deferring the tax he or she will have to pay on the sale.

Tip 83.2: You can try breaking an impasse by having the seller finance the difference between the two prices. You agree to accept his or her price, but ask him or her to agree that the difference not come due for another five years *without interest*. You'll actually be paying less, since inflation will devalue that price during the five-year period, but this option allows the seller to feel he or she has gotten his or her dream price.

Tip 83.3: You can also offer to sign a lease with an option to buy at the seller's price after a set period of time. By the time you have to exercise your option, your affordability will have gone up, as will the value of the house.

Tip 83.4: Another impasse breaker is to ask for added value. Suggest you'll be willing to pay the price the seller wants on the condition the house is painted, or the kitchen remodeled, etc.

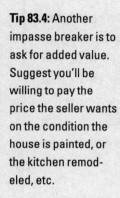

Warning 83.5: Don't let the broker in on any creative financing idea that involves deferred payments. Brokers want their money now and will not be happy campers if they find out they'll have to wait five years for a payment. Their interference is likely to be counterproductive to this negotiation.

84

If the deal fails, don't get upset. If you've negotiated fairly and creatively and the deal still falls through, don't be upset. Deals that fail were meant to fail. Allow yourself a moment to mourn, then take a deep breath, head back to step 54, and resume hunting.

☐ **Done**

85

If you reach an agreement, celebrate . . . for one minute. Congratulations: you've reached a fair deal, and that's the best anyone should hope for in real estate. Take a minute to savor your victory, but only a minute. You've still got lots more work to do before the house is yours.

☐ **Done**

INSPECTING THE HOUSE AND GOING TO CONTRACT

The true heart of the real estate transaction is the contract negotiation, not the price negotiation. And that's not just a lawyer talking. It's the contract that actually spells out who will pay how much to whom and when. I've seen literally hundreds of deals fall apart after both parties shook hands over price. And I've also seen hundreds of otherwise bad deals become good ones by ironing out problems in the contract. But in order to find out if there are any problems to iron out you first need to have the house inspected.

86

Have the house inspected. Yes, you've done your own inspection, but you're not a professional, and before you lay out your hard-earned cash for this house, you want to know just what you're facing. Only a professional inspector will be able to tell if the sag in a roof is a planned drainage feature, or a sign of imminent collapse. Not only will the inspector be able examine all the components that make up the operating systems of the house, but he or she will be able to tell you what repairs have to be made soon after you move in and what those repairs will cost.

☐ **Done**

Warning 86.1: Don't accept the seller or broker's claim that an inspection isn't necessary, even if he or she produces a recent inspection report. And don't hire someone recommended by the seller or broker, either. Rather, look to your attorney for a recommendation.

Tip 86.2: You want someone who does this full-time, who has experience (five to ten years) checking out your specific type of home, and who is a member of a professional society, such as the American Society of Home Inspectors.

Vacation Home Buyer's Tip 86.3 : Inspections are especially important if you're buying in a vacation area, since it's not uncommon for homes in these areas to be exposed to harsh elements, such as desert winds or coastal storms.

Apartment Buyer's Tip 86.4: Home-inspection services will do for most buyers, but if you're in the market for a co-op or condo, you may need to find a licensed engineer who can evaluate the condition and upkeep of the entire building and all its systems.

Tip 86.5: If you're buying from a model in a development before your particular home is completed, hire an inspector to visit the model, then inspect the house as it's being built to make sure the contractor is adhering to the specifications of the model. Yes, this will cost you a bit more, but it just might save you from buying a new but structurally inadequate home that could cause problems down the line.

Tip 86.6: If you're buying a new home, check to see if it's protected by the Home Owners Warranty Corporation (HOW) or one of its competitors. HOW provides ten years of protection against major construction defects, and if one of its 12,500 member-builders refuses to fix a mistake, insurance will cover the repair. HOW policies must be purchased through an active HOW member-builder. A list of their members can be obtained by contacting Public Affairs, HOW, 3774 La Vista Road, Tucker, GA 30084.

87

Ask the inspector for a sample report. Look for thoroughness. If the inspector refuses to provide you with a sample, ask why. If the issue is privacy, allow him or her to black out the name and address.

☐ **Done**

Tip 87.1: Check to see if the sample includes the estimated costs for replacing or repairing the defects in your home. Mention that you'd be willing to pay a higher fee to get these numbers if they are not part of the standard package.

Warning 87.2: There's usually very little room for negotiation when it comes to inspection fees. Most fees run between $100 and $300 and include travel. Depending on real estate and locale, you may have to pay additional fees for termite inspection and water analysis, as well as testing for radon, asbestos, and urea formaldehyde.

88

Accompany the inspector on the search. Ask if you can accompany the inspector on the tour. Most will welcome it. Those who don't are worthy of your suspicion. While accompanying the inspector, feel free to ask questions, but try not to get in the way too much. Watch, listen, and learn.

☐ **Done**

Tip 88.1: If the house is being inspected in winter, some testing might have to be postponed until a thaw. Make sure your contract spells out what obligations the seller will have at that time.

89 **Examine the inspection report.** When you get your inspection report, first make sure you can read it clearly and understand it completely. Remember: there's no such thing as a dumb question.

☐ **Done**

Tip 89.1: When going over the inspection report, keep in mind that the inspection will have centered on the condition of the envelope of the home—roof, walls, windows, and foundation—as well the operating systems—heating, electrical, and plumbing. Don't be surprised if the report includes a disclaimer, saying the findings are based on observable, unconcealed structural conditions. Inspections don't warranty or guarantee the condition of a home, and most reports will say so.

Tip 89.2: It's not uncommon for inspectors' reports to note that they won't be looking for building code violations, nor will they preclude the presence of possible problems with toxic materials, gases, or the presence of chemicals. Inspectors usually check separately for radon and asbestos, and most will do an additional check for termites as well.

Tip 89.3: I insist my clients have both radon and asbestos inspections done as a matter of policy. Both are such potential health hazards that they need to be addressed as quickly as possible. Most mortgage lenders will require a termite inspection as well, since they're concerned about the health of the structure, not you.

Tip 89.4: Once you've interpreted the disclaimers, go to the narrative discussion of the condition of the home, which is usually broken down into separate sections dealing with everything from the foundation to the roof. Read each section, noting the recommendations of the inspector. Underline any mention of repairs that should be made, and when, as well as the possible cost of each.

Tip 89.5: Termite information will be contained within the report on a separate termite certificate. The evaluation will be based on visual evidence, but inaccessibility will be noted.

Tip 89.6: The inspector will summarize his or her observations in a brief abstract that states whether the house is in poor, fair, good, or exceptional condition. Whatever your inspector says, don't take it as a recommendation to

proceed or withdraw from buying the house. All he or she is doing is trying to provide you with the data to make your own informed decision. Remember problems can be addressed in the contract.

Tip 89.7: Make sure you pay close attention to the subtext of the inspection report. Words like "fine," "safe," and "secure" mean just that. Words like "shoddy" and "temporary" are the inspector's subtle way of implying you might be buying a money pit.

90

Study the contract. No standardized contracts for you. As I mentioned, the contract is the heart of the transaction, and as such needs to be customized to fit your wants and needs. This is where your attorney comes in: he or she should study, analyze, and then rewrite the contract, adding clauses to protect your interests. At its most basic, a contract takes the property off the market and spells out the rights and responsibilities of both the seller and the buyer. While the procedure may vary according to what part of the country you live in, in general, it's the seller's attorney or broker who submits the contract. Before you begin hyperventilating, this actually works to your advantage. You and your attorney can now sit back and strike out any objectionable clauses, inserting those of your own. The contract will most likely be sent directly to your attorney; make sure you get a copy as well.

☐ **Done**

Tip 90.1: Whatever you do, don't succumb to pressure by the seller and his or her attorney to hammer out the details of a contract in one afternoon. Take your time, making sure you understand everything contained in the contract and inserting amendments that protect your interests.

Warning 90.2: There's no such thing as a standard contract. The broker's form has been prepared so the broker can make the deal "happen." Beware the broker who assures you the contract is "standard stuff." Standard could be suicidal.

Tip 90.3: Check to make sure the exact location of the home is described as accurately as possible. A mere address is not sufficient. It's best to have either a survey attached, or at least the dimensions of the property.

Apartment Buyer's Tip 90.4: If you're buying a co-op or condo, make sure the apartment number is included. Co-op buyers should also make sure that the number of shares purchased is indicated.

Tip 90.5: The contract should accurately represent the legal status of the home (i.e., one family, two family, etc.). The contract should also stipulate that the seller hand over a certificate of occupancy at the closing. This certificate ensures the home was built according to the municipal building code and zoning regulations. Make sure your attorney has a chance to review the "C of O" well in advance of closing.

Tip 90.6: The purchase price and the exact way it will be paid must be spelled out in the contract. In addition, the contract should state what types of funds will be acceptable as payments for charges: certified checks, bank checks, or cash.

Tip 90.7: Make sure the contract spells out the form of ownership you'll be assuming: individual, joint tenancy, or tenancy in common. Most married couples go for joint tenancy, since it allows ownership to pass from one spouse to the other should one die.

Tip 90.8: Make sure the contract includes a list of personal property included in the sale, and a list of property that isn't. If it's not in the contract, you're not going to get it.

Tip 90.9: Read the entire contract word for word. If there's anything you don't understand, ask your attorney. After all, his or her expertise in these matters is what you're paying for.

91

Amend the contract. After you have studied it along with your lawyer, amend the contract to meet your needs and wants. Remember: the contract sent you was but the first move in a possibly long chess match. You want to come out with at least a draw, if not a win.

☐ **Done**

Tip 91.1: The first item your attorney should customize is the mortgage contingency clause. Make sure there's a provision included that indicates the length of the mortgage you're willing to take, as well as maximum interest rate you'll accept, and that the mortgage commitment be "unconditional." Make sure a specific rate is mentioned and that the mortgage is at the "prevailing rate." This clause should also state the cut-off date for you to get bank approval.

Tip 91.2: Clauses should be included that force the seller to maintain the landscaping and walk as well as the house itself before closing. There should also be a stipulation that the house be turned over in "broom clean" condition: in other words, *sans* garbage or any other mess.

Tip 91.3: A clause should stipulate the seller's liability for any damage to the home resulting from floods, fire, wind, rain, or hurricane. You want a guarantee that you'll receive the home in the condition it was in when the contract was signed. The clause should state that the seller must bring his insurance up to "replacement cost" for the home—this protects you should the house need to be rebuilt in case of fire.

Tip 91.4: The contract will make clear exactly how much of a deposit is due upon signing, as well as what the deposit should consist of. Most contracts specify putting down 10 percent of the total price of the house in cash. If you're short, offer 5 percent now and 5 percent thirty to sixty days later.

Warning 91.5: Don't settle for a contract that gives you the right to take back your deposit only if the title proves faulty. Make sure you're entitled to have your legal fees paid as well as any other out-of-pocket expenses (title search, cost of inspection) incurred should the seller default.

Tip 91.6: The contract should stipulate that all escrow accounts are interest bearing. Make sure that attorneys or title company representatives hold the moneys. The contract should also state that the eventual recipient of the moneys receives the interest.

Warning 91.7: Brokers, sellers, or lawyers may try to convince you that as the buyer, you're responsible for paying all closing costs. You can negotiate who will pay for what and have it written into the contract.

Tip 91.8: Make sure the contract allows for an inspection several days before the date of closing, so you're assured of getting the house—structure and building systems—in the condition agreed upon. Include another clause that allows for an inspection on closing day itself. This gives the seller a chance to remedy any problem. If there's a problem at closing, the only way to ensure it will be taken care of is to hold money out from the purchase price and place it in escrow until the work is done.

Tip 91.9: While a date and time of closing must be written into every contract, there are three ways in which this info can be listed: "on," "on or about," and "time is of the essence." Instruct your attorney to change any "time is of the essence" language to "on or about" language. Sellers may have a fit, but that's too bad. This change protects you from default should anything prevent you from closing on the stipulated date.

Tip 91.10: Be sure your attorney changes each mention of the number of days you have to take an action to the same number of business days.

Tip 91.11: A clause should be added that insists the house be delivered vacant.

Tip 91.12: If you're buying a brand-new home from a developer, sponsor, or builder, add a clause stating that the plumbing, roof, and other systems are guaranteed for at least a year after title closing. The seller should also agree to return and make repairs if problems arise. Be sure the contract includes an outside date for closing and occupancy, as well as a provision stating that the seller will provide you with a duplicate mortgage if there are any delays and your mortgage expires, making it impossible for you to get a new one at the same or lower rate. Make sure that if you can't close or take occupancy by a certain date, you can cancel the deal and get back your deposits, fees, charges, and expenses.

92

Sign the contract and cele-brate . . . for one minute.
Remember that the contract negotiation, like the price negotiation, is a game of give and take. You probably won't be able to get everything you want. Trust your attorney's judgment whether or not to sign or walk away. Having signed, celebrate . . . but only for a minute. You're not done yet. You have to get a mortgage.

☐ **Done**

GETTING A MORTGAGE

Though it might seem like an over-whelming, not to mention frightening, prospect, securing a good mortgage isn't too difficult—if the lender sees you and your financial history in the best possible light. Keep in mind that the lender has three priorities when it comes to giving you money: your willingness to pay back the loan, your ability to pay it back, and the value of the collateral offered to secure the loan. Meet all three and you'll get your money. But first, you've got to get your financial house in tip-top order.

93

Check your own credit report. This gives you a chance to correct and clean it up before the banker sets eyes on it. Contact TRW, Trans Union, or Equifax, whichever credit bureau covers your area, and find out how to get a copy of your report. You're entitled to it by law. The usual procedure is for you to write a letter requesting your report. Include your full name, address (for the last five years), and Social Security number. Some of the bureaus offer consumers one free report per year, and if you've been denied credit within the past thirty days, you're entitled to obtain one copy free of charge. Otherwise, be prepared to pay $5 to $15 for the report.

☐ **Done**

94

Study the report. Each entry, called a "trade line," details either a request for info about your credit or an action taken by a granter of credit regarding your account with them. Granters usually qualify your status with them through the use of a code.

☐ **Done**

Warning 94.1: It's not uncommon for credit reports to contain errors—errors that can mean thumbs down to your getting a mortgage. For that reason, go over your credit report very carefully. Any error you catch and correct now can make the difference between owning your own home or just dreaming about it.

Warning 94.2: The head of the bank won't be reading your report—a clerk will—and he or she will usually just scan the report looking for some overall trend in your credit granters' feelings about you. A series of Non or Neg ratings could mean curtains when it comes to getting a mortgage.

95

If you find an error in your credit report, address it immediately. Send a letter to the bureau detailing your discovery. State that you want the information verified and that if they aren't able to do so, you want it removed from your report. Most credit bureaus allot fifteen business days to verify entries. If, within that time, they cannot come up with the info to verify what is in your report, they will remove it from your file.

☐ **Done**

Tip 95.1: If you have any pertinent information backing up your claim, send it along with your letter. Make sure to send copies, not the originals.

Tip 95.2: Sometimes the terminology used by credit granters can be changed if you offer legitimate reasons for slow payment. Press the granter, not the credit bureau, for the correction/elimination of any negative wording that appears in your report. Make sure the granter sends notification to the credit bureau to change your status or code.

Tip 95.3: If the changes you've requested won't show up on the report before the banker sees it, tell him or her you've taken action to clean up your credit file, and show copies of all the correspondence.

Tip 95.4: Insist that corrected versions of your credit report be sent to anyone who in the past year requested and received a copy containing the incorrect information.

96

If necessary, add a 100-word statement to your report. If, after working to get corrections made, your report still details a negative or ambiguous tone or details a sequence of negative events that reflect poorly or ambiguously on your current financial situation, take the next step and address this interpretation. By law, you're allowed to have a 100-word consumer statement attached to your credit report to clarify entries. Your statement can counteract negative statements with explanations putting the event into context. For example: explain how your slow payment record in 1993 was the result of your having to undergo surgery. Show how you "cured" the problem, either by paying back due amounts or making double payments.

☐ **Done**

Tip 96.1: Request that this consumer statement become a permanent part of your credit report. By law, it must be included if you request it.

97

Explore your mortgage options. There are numerous types of mortgages available today. Look for one that meets your specific needs.

☐ **Done**

Tip 97.1: Start by exploring thirty-year fixed-rate mortgages (FRMs). Historically the most common type of mortgage, FRMs are those in which the interest rate charge is fixed for the entire term of the mortgage. The advantage is obvious: your monthly payment of interest and principal remain the same for the life of the mortgage, guaranteeing stability in an often volatile market. But that stability comes at a price: the down payment required can be steep, and you'll also have to face the fact that interest on fixed loans tends to be higher than that on adjustable loans.

Warning 97.2: While amortization costs remain static over the term of an FRM, monthly payments can increase if taxes and insurance costs are part of the payment.

Tip 97.3: The fifteen-year fixed rate mortgage permits you to own your home in half the time, and for less than half the total interest cost of a thirty-year loan. However, since your monthly payments will be higher, these loans are more difficult to qualify for.

Tip 97.4: Explore thirty-year adjustable-rate mortgages (ARMs), in which interest rates—and therefore the size of your monthly payment—rise and fall with market conditions, based on an index used by the lender. ARMs are good for individuals who expect to own three or more

homes over the course of their lives, since the up-front points that have to be paid at closing are lower than those of an FRM. They're potentially danger-ous for those who need predictable monthly expenses. Some ARMs offer a negative amortization feature, which allows the lender to add the increased cost of rising interest rates on to the unpaid principal of the loan, rendering monthly payments fixed and predictable. But there's a down side to such ARMs: your total indebtedness can increase over time, cutting into your equity.

Warning 97.5: Beware of "discount ARMs," which are offered at initial rates below the sum of the margin and the index. The introductory rate lasts until the first adjustment period, as set down in the contract. Unfortunately, these loans tend to be combined with initial loan fees that are quite sizable, dramatically increasing their real cost.

Tip 97.6: If you've got a spotless credit record and will be able to make a sizable down payment, check out "no-doc" loans, which require little to no documentation to secure.

Some lenders who offer these boast of their ability to offer binding loan commitments in under an hour.

Tip 97.7: Graduated payment mortgages (GPMs) start out with low payments, then rise gradually and eventually level off. The advantage of the initially lower payments is that they enable buyers to qualify for a larger mortgage loan than usual. The disadvantage is that initial low payments aren't enough to cover fully the interest due on the loan, so the difference is added to the balance. Thus, future interest payments are based upon the new, higher loan balance, making those payments mighty high.

Tip 97.8: Growing equity mortgages (GEMs) have payments that increase for a fixed number of years, then level off. The borrower saves on total interest costs, and the interest rates charged for this kind of mortgage may be lower than for longer-term mortgages. You should consider this type of mortgage only if you're positive your income will be able to keep pace with increasing payments.

Tip 97.9: If you're a vet, see if you're eligible for a Veterans Administration (VA) loan. These have fixed rates with long repayment periods. The interest rate is set by the VA; in most cases, low down payments are required, unless you're angling for a loan with a graduated payment feature. These loans can be paid off in full at any time without threat of penalty. In addition, the VA collects a one-time funding fee of 1 percent of the loan amount at settlement. Your local VA office can give you information on eligibility.

Tip 97.10: It could be worth your while to see if you can qualify for a Federal Housing Authority (FHA) insured loan. These loans are offered by institutional lenders (including savings institutions, commercial banks, and mortgage companies) that are guaranteed by the federal government. They generally carry interest rates below market, but since the rate is not set by the FHA, you must still shop around. And though these loans can take longer to process than conventional loans, there are some definite perks.

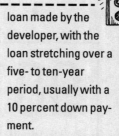

loan made by the developer, with the loan stretching over a five- to ten-year period, usually with a 10 percent down payment.

Retirement Home Buyer's Tip 97.12: Don't let your age keep you from taking out a long-term mortgage. My eighty-year-old parents took out a thirty-year mortgage to buy their retirement home. Banks won't have a problem with your taking out a mortgage longer than your presumed life span since they assume the cost will be paid when the estate sells the property upon your death. Besides, I believe mortgages are life extenders.

Vacation Home Buyer's Warning 97.11: Be aware that it's very difficult to get a mortgage for a time share. Most financing is usually done through a personal

98

Compile a list of lenders who offer the type of mortgage you're looking for. Compile a list of all the financial institutions in your area offering mortgages, including commercial banks, mortgage bankers, credit unions, savings and loans, insurance companies, savings banks, and even credit card companies. Comparison shopping will be crucial, since some banks have more generous loan-to-value and income ratios, making them more available to you.

☐ **Done**

Vacation Home Buyer's Tip 98.1: Check with larger banks in your area to see if they offer what are called "second primary home" loans. These are available to individuals who: have a net worth of over $100,000; a debt-to-income ratio of no more than 40 percent; and are buying a second home no more than three hours from their primary home.

Vacation Home Buyer's Tip 98.2: If you don't qualify for a "second primary home" loan, turn to smaller local banks in the area in which your second home is to be purchased. More often than not, they're more amenable than larger distant lenders.

Tip 98.3: Check the Yellow Pages to see if there's a mortgage compilation service in your area. These services sell a list of lenders and what they're offering, which can make comparison shopping a whole lot easier. The lists are usually updated weekly. If you live in a large metropolitan area, one of the newspapers in town is bound to publish the weekly rates in either the real estate or weekly business section. You can use this as well, since the data is usually supplied by a mortgage compilation service.

99

Call each institution on your list and ask to speak to a loan officer about mortgages. Once you get him or her on the phone, be pleasant. You're going to have to ask a long series of questions.

☐ **Done**

Tip 99.1: If you're interested in a fixed-rate mortgage, ask what the interest rate is, how long the term is, what the aggregate points are, and what the annual percentage rate, or APR is.

Tip 99.2: If you're interested in adjustable-rate mortgages, find out: rates, terms, and points; what the change period is, and what the maximum allowable change is for the period, and over the life of the loan; whether or not the loan can be converted to a fixed-rate instrument in the future without considerable expense; and what index is being used as a basis in adjusting the rate.

Tip 99.3: For all loans, ask what the maximum loan amount is, and check to see if the type of dwelling has any bearing on the rate charged. Make sure you find out how long it will take the lender to approve your loan application.

Tip 99.4: Make sure you ask the loan officer about the lender's loan-to-value ratio requirement and income ratio (the maximum percentage of monthly gross income it believes someone should allocate for shelter). There's no reason for a lender to be secretive about these numbers. If the loan officer refuses to disclose this information, ask to speak to his or her supervisor. If you're still stonewalled, find another lender.

Tip 99.5: Ask what the total amount of all fees comes to—including appraisal, lender's attorney, credit check, and application. Find out if the lender's loans carry any prepayment penalties, as well as what they are and when they occur.

Tip 99.6: Don't forget to ask the loan officer about any special programs the lender offers to existing customers. See if the lender has programs that can expedite the decision-making process, such as no-income-verification loans. NIV may speed the loan process, but it'll cost you: rates are usually one-eighth of a point higher.

Tip 99.7: Find out the lender's mortgage commitment policies, inquiring how long the commitment is good for. Find out if renewals are available and at what rate. Ask whether or not the lender locks in the interest rate at the time of application, or if it remains variable until closing.

Retirement Home Buyer's Tip 99.8: If you're an older American buying your last home, ask about obtaining a mortgage that has no prepayment penalties. That way you can get out easily if you discover you've made a mistake.

100

Decide which lender is right for you, then pick up a mortgage application.

Most applications are the same in that they'll want to know: your gross salary; current address; whether you rent or own; the length of time you've been living at that address, as well as any other addresses you've lived at in the previous five years; a listing of all your assets and all your obligations. If it seems like an awful lot of information to provide, you're right, it is. But there's a reason for it: the bank is trying to gauge not only your ability to pay, but your character as well. Their analysis is based on a scoring system wherein they assign a numeric value to the answers you give on your application. Score above a certain number and you'll get your mortgage. Score below and you'll be turned down.

☐ **Done**

Tip 100.1: To beat the system, refrain from providing a simple answer to any question that might adversely affect your score. Instead, insert a note requesting the reader to see a supplement you've attached. Use the supplement to explain or rationalize your answer, framing it in positive terms.

Tip 100.2: To the lender, answers to questions about your current residence and job situation are important measures of stability. Supplement your answer here by noting that while you might have resided in a different apartment every year, or held down a variety of jobs, each has been a step up, reflecting career stability and growth.

Tip 100.3: If you've worked less than three years at your current job, supplement your answer with a list of previous jobs and/or school attendance that shows you have steadily advanced in your career and salary with each move.

Tip 100.4: If you're self-employed, supplement your 1040 form with a profit-and-loss statement, or a letter prepared by your accountant. Detail any long-term contracts and business arrangements that indicate your income source is stable.

Tip 100.5: Provide a supplement for the "other income" section of the application, indicating interest from savings accounts, income from securities, rents received, and annual cash gifts. Make sure you include moneys obtained from reasonable expectations, such as salary raises, annual bonuses, and debt repayments. The cessation of a student loan payment, for example, qualifies as an addition to your income. Anything you can add to this supplement will greatly add to your cause.

101 **Find someone who can shepherd your application through the red tape.** To do this, put on your finest duds and head out to the lender's offices, application in hand. Ask to speak to someone in the mortgage department. Tell the person that yours is a special mortgage application, and that you worked very hard on it. Show him or her the supplements attached, together with your credit file and the documented evidence of the steps you undertook to cleanse it. Ask your contact to keep an eye on your application, and ask him or her if you can call if you have any questions. If all goes according to plan, you'll have your commitment papers within five weeks.

☐ **Done**

Tip 101.1: If your application is rejected, find out why. Federal law states that any mortgage loan rejection must give a specific reason for the decision. Once you know why you were rejected, you can concentrate on clearing up that problem.

Tip 101.2: Call the lender's mortgage department and find out what the appeals process is. If one exists, follow it exactly. If there is no appeals process, create one. Call up the head of the lender's mortgage division and set up a meeting. Ask for his or her help,

indicating that you understand the lender's need for protection, but that you have the capacity to pay the loan back, as well as the character and collateral to pay back on time. Supply the lender with new supplements and a reworked application. If you have to show additional income, bring in a guarantor or get a part-time job. Don't be afraid to push the up button if you don't get satisfaction. At the same time you're pursuing your appeal, begin the application process with another lender. Remember that it was your mortgage application that was rejected—not you.

102

Make a photocopy of your mortgage commitment from the lender and send it to your attorney. The two of you should carefully review it together, making sure it matches the description given you over the telephone when you first got in touch with the lender. If there's anything you don't understand, have the attorney explain it to you. If there's anything he or she isn't clear on, call the lender. Only when you're totally satisfied with the terms of the commitment and aware of all the conditions should you sign.

☐ **Done**

103

Celebrate . . . for more than a minute. Now is the time to break out the bubbly, since the hardest work is over and the biggest hurdles cleared. While you're not home free—there's still the move and the closing—allow yourself to take a weekend off to start dreaming about your new home before you move on to Stage 8.

☐ **Done**

MOVING AND CLOSING

These final two steps in the home-buying process, while fairly straightforward, still have the potential for disaster. There's nothing worse than a screwup on the day of closing when you're poised to move in and have no place else to go. Unless, of course, it's your possessions arriving damaged . . . or not arriving at all.

104

Sort through your possessions. Having bought a home, you now need to realize that every object you take with you to that home will cost you money either in storage or moving costs. Decide what you'll be taking with you and what you're willing to part with.

☐ **Done**

105

Consider holding a tag sale.
If you're parting with a considerable amount of property, consider holding a tag sale. While you'll never get as much money from such a sale as you'd wish, whatever you do make will defray the cost of moving or storing everything you're keeping.

☐ **Done**

Tip 105.1: Hire a professional tag-sale company rather than trying to run the sale yourself. These companies are not only knowledgeable about pricing, presentation, and publicity, but they have their own clientele. This is one situation where you're better off leaving it to the experts.

106 Contact moving companies. Call three local companies that are part of national franchises and have them come and give you estimates.

☐ **Done**

Tip 106.1: Ask each moving company for a binding estimate. In most cases, movers will agree to provide you with a binding estimate that they won't exceed but that will be lowered if they've overestimated the weight of your possessions. They are required to give you a binding estimate if the move is interstate.

Tip 106.2: Speak with your insurance broker about whether or not you need extra coverage. Ask for a recommendation on whether you should buy supplemental coverage from the mover or on your own.

Tip 106.3: Have the mover do most of the packing for you. Not only are movers more adept at packing than you are, since they do it nearly every day, but if they pack something and it breaks they're liable for the damage— whereas if you pack it and it breaks, they're not. It's also a big time-saver. Use your time to look for new furniture rather than wrapping your spoon collection in newspaper and searching for cardboard boxes.

107

**Check on the movers' reputa-
tions.** Call your local Better
Business Bureau and ask
them if there have been any complaints
about the three movers you've contacted
and how they've been resolved. The moving business is an easy one to enter and
has more than its share of con artists.

☐ **Done**

Tip 107.1: Agree on a method of payment before signing your moving agreement. Most movers will accept cash, money orders, traveler's checks, cashier checks—but *not* personal checks. Some will even take credit cards.

Tip 107.2: Be sure any moving agreement you sign states specific dates for pickup and delivery. Don't schedule moving days too close to your final days in your old home or to the first day of ownership in your new home. Inability to accept delivery could result in the mover's placing your valued possessions in storage, then charging a warehouse fee based on how much space your goods occupy.

108

Complete all personal paper work for the move. Begin by contacting your local school district and arranging to have your children's records transferred. Get change-of-address cards from the post office and send them to magazines, credit card companies, and any other organizations that regularly send you mail. While there, fill out a forwarding request so your mail follows you to your new abode. Once home, call the telephone and utility companies and arrange for a date to have service disconnected in your old home and connected in your new. Call the department of motor vehicles and have automobile records updated to reflect your new address. Have all bank accounts transferred to a new bank or a different branch of the same bank. Cancel the newspaper and arrange for delivery at your new home. Defrost and dry out refrigerators and freezers in preparation for the move. Pack small valuable objects and important papers yourself, and bring them in the car with you and your family. (If the movers do the packing, make sure you weed this stuff out prior to packing day.)

☐ **Done**

109

Make sure you have adequate insurance in the new home. This seems pretty obvious, although some buyers find themselves surprised when the mortgagee at closing requires them to show a comprehensive policy that at the very least covers the mortgage. In fact, the policy should list the mortgagee as a beneficiary in addition to you and your family. The policy should cover the replacement value of the home itself as well as the contents inside. Some policies include public liability insurance—to protect you in case anyone is injured on your property—as well as other variations.

☐ **Done**

Apartment Buyer's Tip 109.1: Insurance for a condo or co-op is different in that one major policy covers the entire complex. Part of your monthly maintenance fee, therefore, includes a prorated share of the premium. However, you'll need your own policy to cover your individual unit's contents.

Tip 109.2: It's worth checking into special types of insurance if you're going to be living in an area threatened by floods. The federal government has established the National Flood Insurance Program to protect areas from flooding, storms, or hurricanes.

110

Arrange for your preclosing walk-through. Arduous though it may sound, your preclosing walk-through should be done with a fine-tooth comb, the better to ward off any future headaches or complications. For example: if your walk-through reveals furniture that hasn't been removed, tell your attorney; why should you spend your hard-earned cash to have their junk removed? Similarly, if the seller says he or she would like to stay in the house a few days past closing, stop right there and have your attorney draw up a possession agreement stating that, in lieu of rent, you get a per-diem reduction in the purchase price. In the case of any other last-minute glitches, have your attorney draw up an agreement that requires the seller to take care of it and place money from the purchase price in escrow. Make sure it's an interest-bearing instrument and that the eventual recipient receives the interest.

☐ **Done**

Tip 110.1: Don't hesitate to bring any serious problems to the seller's attention. Sometimes things don't come to light until furniture and fixtures have been removed.

111

Check the mover's inventory.
Before the moving truck pulls out of the driveway with your goods, make sure you understand any notations the mover has made on his inventory. If you don't agree with the mover's assessment of the condition of any item, note your objection on the inventory list. Do not sign the list until you've read it carefully and made any corrections.

☐ **Done**

112

Ask your attorney to arrange a preclosing. For the most part, closings are pretty straightforward, since everything that goes on has already been agreed upon in the contract. But things can—and do—go wrong. That's why it's in your interest to be as informed and prepared as possible. A preclosing—in which you and your attorney sit down and run through it, step by step—is a good way to familiarize yourself with the closing process. Have the attorney find out exactly what every charge will be, and have him or her explain all fees. The attorney should also have copies of all the documents you'll have to sign so you can truly read them.

☐ **Done**

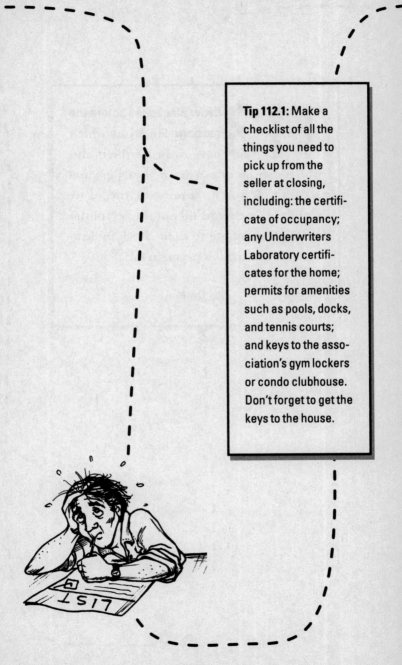

Tip 112.1: Make a checklist of all the things you need to pick up from the seller at closing, including: the certificate of occupancy; any Underwriters Laboratory certificates for the home; permits for amenities such as pools, docks, and tennis courts; and keys to the association's gym lockers or condo clubhouse. Don't forget to get the keys to the house.

113

Draw all checks before the closing. Find out which have to be certified and which can be drawn from your personal account. If you're unsure of the exact amount of a charge, fill out the rest of the check. Clip a note to each check indicating exactly what it is payment for.

☐ **Done**

Tip 113.1: If possible, have checks for adjustments made out before closing as well. Adjustments, or prorations, are the payments you'll be making for the fuel remaining in the seller's oil tank, or the property taxes paid last month, etc. They can be tricky to calculate, and have been known to derail exchange of title. Taking care of it in advance is the way to go.

Apartment Buyer's Tip 113.2: If you're buying a co-op, you may have to pay an additional set of fees that include credit investigation, as well as processing and application charges that must be paid to the building's managing agent. You may also be required to pay a flip tax—an extraordinary fee charged by the co-op corporation to enhance its financial reserves. Condos may require you to pay a month's worth of common charges as an additional security deposit. Many multifamily dwellings ask for deposits when you move in, just in case you dent the elevator door or scratch the banister.

114

Go to closing. Make sure you bring the checks you've predrawn as well as some blanks (just in case), a copy of the reconciliation statement, identification, and a copy of your loan commitment letter. Be prepared to feel a little overwhelmed as you hand over check after check after check. But when you take the key to your new home and open the front door for the first time, knowing that the house is yours, you'll know it's all been worth it.

☐ **Done**

Warning 114.1: Don't be surprised if, at the closing, the lender's representative tries to sell you mortgage life insurance, offering a policy that covers the unpaid portion of the mortgage and features an apparently reasonable premium. Tell him or her you'll pass: you can get better coverage for less money by taking out a "reducing term" life insurance policy in the amount of the mortgage.

115

Have the mover's payment ready. Be prepared for the mover to demand his or her payment before the crew unloads so much as an ashtray at your new house. If you have any valued possessions, consider tipping before the crew unloads them.

☐ **Done**

116 **Check for obvious damage to your possessions once they're in your new home.** If you discover something has been broken, leave the damaged item in the packaging so an agent from the company can take a look at it. Claim forms must be filed within nine months of a move and are available from the moving company's home office or agent.

☐ **Done**

117

Relax. You've done it! You're in your new home, surrounded by your possessions and loved ones. Enjoy it for as long as you can. If you're like most other homeowners, pretty soon you're going to start thinking about renovation projects.

☐ **Done**

GLOSSARY

adjournment: An agreement to shift a meeting or proceeding, in this case a title closing, to a later date or time.

adjustable-rate mortgages (ARMs): Mortgages in which interest rates rise and fall based on an index selected by the lender.

affordability: A judgment on how much you can afford to spend on a purchase; in the case of a home this consists of how much you can spend monthly on a mortgage payment.

apartment: An individual living unit in a building that consists of many such units; can be either rented or purchased, and may vary in size from one room to more than ten.

association: A form of real estate ownership in which individuals own their own building and the land it stands on, but share ownership of a communal recreation area—such as a beach, park, lake, or golf course—with other individual owners.

attached house: A structure, designed as the home for a single family, that shares one or two walls with similar structures; common examples are town houses, row houses, and brownstones.

binding estimate: A price quote on the cost of a move in which the mover agrees the final cost will not exceed the stated amount; while often slightly higher than other types of estimates, it ensures you won't be surprised when you're handed the bill.

boilerplate: Standard legal language, used in formal documents, that while important, is rarely changed by either party since it has become the accepted form in the legal and commercial community.

closing: The meeting at which the final formalities for the sale of real estate are concluded, after which the buyer takes ownership and usually possession.

commission: The payment to a broker or brokerage agency for help in selling a home; typically paid by the seller; the going rate is 6 percent of the selling price; however, it is entirely negotiable.

comparables or "comps": Recently sold houses and apartments, similar in age, size, style, condition, and/or location to the one in question, which can be used as a basis of comparison for determining price; the more recent the "comp," and the closer it resembles the home, the better its comparability.

condominium or "condo": A form of real estate ownership in which individuals own their living units, but share ownership of common facilities—lawns, gardens, halls, elevators, etc.—with the owners of other units.

cooperative or "co-op": A form of real estate ownership in which individuals own shares in a corporation which owns the entire structure.

deed: A document transferring the legal title of real estate from one person to another.

detached single family house: A structure, situated on its own piece of land, designed as the home for a single family.

fee simple: A form of real estate ownership in which individuals own both the building and the property it stands on.

financing: The means by which a buyer will be paying the agreed price on a home if he or she doesn't have sufficient cash.

fixed-rate mortgages (FRMs): Mortgages in which the interest rate charged is fixed for the entire term of the mortgage.

graduated payment mortgages (GPMs): Mortgages that start off with low payments that then rise gradually, eventually leveling off.

growing equity mortgages (GEMs): Mortgages with payments that increase for a fixed number of years and then level off.

listing: The detailed physical description of a home that will be presented to potential buyers.

mortgage: A loan by which the borrower gives the lender a lien on real estate as security for the repayment of the loan; the borrower has use of the real estate and the lien is removed when the loan is paid in full.

mortgage compilation services: Services that compile a list of area mortgage lenders, their products, and the terms of their offerings, making comparison shopping much easier.

mortgage contingency: A clause in a contract for the sale of real estate that links the buyer's obligation to purchase the real estate to his or her ability to obtain a mortgage. The exact language and restrictiveness of the clause are open to negotiation.

mortgagee: The lender issuing a mortgage on a parcel of real estate; the borrower is called the mortgagor.

multifamily house: A structure designed to house two or three families; typically one of the units is occupied by the owner while the other(s) is rented.

no-documentation mortgages: Mortgages that require little or no documentation to secure; usually requiring spotless credit records and sizable down payments.

no-income-verification mortgages: Mortgages that don't require verification of income but usually carry higher rates as a result.

partnership: A form of real estate ownership in which two or more unrelated individuals share ownership of a single home or unit.

payoff letter: A document, prepared by a mortgage holder ahead of time but completed at the closing, which documents that a mortgage has indeed been paid off and that the buyer or his or her mortgage holder, can now obtain title.

radon: Produced by decaying uranium, radon is a colorless and odorless radioactive gas that exists naturally in soil and rock; it has been linked to lung cancer; while it diffuses quickly in the open air, if it seeps into a home it can accumulate to potentially dangerous levels.

second primary home loans: Special loans made on the purchase of second homes located no more than three hours from primary homes; obviously used for weekend homes rather than true vacation homes.

terms: The stipulations and details of an agreement, including the selling price and financing arrangements.

time shares: A form of owning real estate in which ownership is divided into fifty-two parts, each of which is sold off one or more at a time; each owner is entitled to use of the property for a certain number of weeks of the year; typically found in vacation areas where homes aren't used

by a family for more than one or two
weeks per year.

title: The legal right to ownership of real
estate, or alternatively, a document grant-
ing it.

title company: A company that researches
and issues a report on the legal status of
the title, or ownership, of a property; the
report describes the property and demon-
strates who owns it and whether or not
there are any title defects, liens, or
encumbrances that would interfere with
ownership being transferred; title companies also offer insurance protection to
both owners and lenders, and in some
states, may handle the entire closing.

title issues: Any matters, such as title
defects, liens, or encumbrances, that
could interfere with the passing title to
the buyer.

underwriting ratios: The financial formula
used by a lender to determine whether or
not it will underwrite, or assume the risk,
of making the loan; these formulas vary
from lender to lender.